HOW TO
SURVIVE
AMERICA

ALSO BY D.L. HUGHLEY

Surrender, White People!
How Not to Get Shot
Black Man, White House

HOW TO SURVIVE AMERICA

D.L. HUGHLEY

AND DOUG MOE

MARINER BOOKS

Boston   New York

HarperCollins books may be purchased for educational, business, or sales promotional use. For information, please email the Special Markets Department at SPsales@harpercollins.com.

A hardcover edition of this book was published in 2021 by Custom House, an imprint of William Morrow.

FIRST MARINER PAPERBACK EDITION PUBLISHED 2022.

Designed by Lucy Albanese

Library of Congress Cataloging-in-Publication Data has been applied for.

ISBN 978-0-06-307276-3

22 23 24 25 26   LSC   10 9 8 7 6 5 4 3 2 1

Although this book is called *How to Survive America*,
it is dedicated to all those who didn't! Rest well.

CONTENTS

HOW TO
SURVIVE
AMERICA

INTRODUCTION

AMERICA'S CHRONIC ILLNESS

How do we survive America?

The media's gonna think I'm being a button-pushing comedian for asking that question so bluntly. But I'm dead serious: Black and brown folks are in a battle for *survival* every damn day in this country, in a way white people can't fully comprehend.

Our life expectancy is a full three *years* less than white Americans. The very air we breathe is more polluted, our water is more contaminated, our local food options are toxic, and our jobs are underpaid. Folks where I grew up in South Central L.A. aren't jogging to the local Whole

Foods for a smoothie. Even if they could afford it, odds are they'd have early stage lung cancer by the time they got there. Black people have higher rates of obesity, high blood pressure, and other risk factors, owing in no small part to adverse environmental factors. Despite the obvious need, the quality of our health care is tragically inadequate. According to the American Cancer Society, African Americans have the *highest* death rate from most cancers and the lowest survival length. Our kidneys fail us at three times the rate of whites. Damn, even our kidneys are profiling us.

Still alive? Well, even the healthiest among us gotta be careful out there. Our communities are statistically less safe than the average, and yet we're terrorized by the law-enforcement and criminal-justice systems that are supposed to protect us, sending us to prison at five times the rate of whites. Not least, our means of addressing these injustices—*voting*—is perennially under assault.

It's enough to drive you crazy. Well, guess what? According to Cigna, we're 20 percent more likely to report "psychological distress" yet "50 percent less likely to receive counseling or mental health treatment." It's almost like the entire country has been structured to kill us. *Hmmm.*

So, I ask the question again: How do we survive America?

■ ■ ■

These are perilous times. I began writing this book in 2020. George Floyd's execution by a white police officer on May 25, 2020, once again spotlighted the systemic racism and police violence that has plagued Black Americans for more than four hundred years. The uncontrolled spread of the coronavirus has devastated the entire country, claiming half a million lives, but disproportionately killing Black and brown Americans. And our government's reaction was to double down on policies that make the problems worse. Even when the vaccines arrived, we got vaccinated at a lower rate than the rest of America, despite being higher risk.

Right now, in America, Black people are less healthy, earn less money, and have less money saved than white people. And police keep arresting more Black Americans, keep stopping more Black drivers, and keep killing more Black Americans than white Americans.

Who's to blame?

The answer, dear reader, is shocking. I couldn't believe it myself. It's like the twist at the end of an M. Night Shyamalan movie: the killer is *us*. It's a classic whodunnit. The bad news is: *we done it*.

In America, Black people are the number one suspects

in our own demise. Whatever bad thing happens to us, it's because Black people are predisposed to that outcome.

At least that's what white people would have you believe. If you turn on the news, listen to the pundits and the politicians, it's the message you hear explicitly and when you read between the lines: *you Black people did this to yourselves.*

It's the same old story since the beginning of this country: Black people in America are predisposed toward ruin. No matter what happens to us, it was our fault. If Black people are slaves, it must be our fault. If police continue to brutalize us, it must be our fault. If Black Americans die from COVID at higher rates, it must be our fault. From the Founding Fathers until now, we're always at fault. We're built for it. We're culpable for it.

Ahmaud Arbery didn't die from being hunted down by gun-toting vigilantes; he died from attacking the gunman. George Floyd didn't die from a police officer kneeling on his neck; he had preexisting conditions. If you lost your job, if you got sick, if you don't have money: it's your own damn fault.

And that's because Black Americans are suspect. We're culturally corrupt, socially corrupt, and immoral.

Or we gotta be, right? Otherwise, how can you explain

all the continued injustice? How can you explain the way we've been treated? If a Black guy gets killed by the police, he must have been to blame for his own death in some way! Because if he wasn't, that would mean that the whole system is fucked up.

White people bend over backward to not be held accountable for the system that they set up and perpetuate. They elected Donald Trump and then excused his racism at every turn and enabled his lies, because they are comfortable in these lies. For four hundred years, white people have told themselves lies to smooth over uncomfortable truths. They've lied to perpetuate white supremacy and preserve their dominance over Black lives. They've justified their cruelty and victimization of Black people by painting Black people as immoral, genetically defective, predisposed to be weak of mind and character. To be more fit to live as slaves than to live as free men. And once free, to stay second-class citizens.

But it wasn't until George Floyd's death that a lot of white Americans were willing to look at the disease America is afflicted with. Maybe it had something to do with everyone being quarantined during the COVID crisis and having nothing to watch on TV. *Oh, there's no more* Real

Housewives? *Let's see what's on Twitter . . . Oh shit, what the fuck is this?!*

America is sick. That much is clear. Because when a white police officer is willing to put his knee on a guy's neck and choke him to death on camera, all the while with people pleading with him to stop, what else can you call it but a disease? If it's just "a few bad apples," how come we keep seeing all these bad apples all the time? Maybe the whole fucking bushel is bad, right?

But Black people have known this. We've been saying this for years. The police are the way they are because they've been built that way. They are predisposed to be violent toward Black people, to humiliate them, to dominate and abuse them. George Floyd's death was caught on tape, but so many others have been too. How many of these videos do we have to see to confirm that the rot is core-deep?

It wasn't too long ago that we were all living in "postracial America" instead of "pro-racist America." I thought Obama changed everything? His election was supposed to be proof that we had entered a future of racial harmony, that the forces of bigotry and racism had been overcome. Remember when John McCain was confronted by a woman who said that Obama was some kind of secret Muslim terrorist and he pushed back on her, insisting that Obama was a "decent family man"? It was a new era.

And Obamacare got passed! Millions of people finally had access to health care, and Americans could no longer be denied health insurance for having preexisting conditions.

Unfortunately, Obama wasn't the end of racism in America because all the Obamacare in the world couldn't fix America's main preexisting condition: racism. In fact, even Obama himself says in his new book, *A Promised Land*, that he thinks his presidency brought up entrenched fears of Black people, exacerbating tensions: "It was as if my very presence in the White House had triggered a deep-seated panic, a sense that the natural order had been disrupted. . . . For millions of Americans spooked by a Black man in the White House, [Trump] promised an elixir for their racial anxiety." Obama's administration sucker-punched a lot of white people and drove them crazy. Trump's election was the expression of this white anxiety. What Black people are actually suffering from is not a predisposition, but a preexisting condition: racism. Racism is America's chronic illness and white supremacy, not Black inferiority, is the cause.

Now America has to decide if she's going to take her medicine.

We gotta put America under the microscope. Because maybe now is finally the time that white people can listen to a diagnosis they might not like. Damn, I wish it hadn't taken Trump fucking up our country and killing more than five hundred thousand people, but maybe now they'll listen. When you go to the doctor, you describe your symptoms and get an examination. If you're lucky, maybe you just get an X-ray. Worst case, the doctor grabs your junk and makes you cough. Or he puts his finger up your butt. Yeah, it can get nasty. But America can keep on having problems, or we can try to fix shit right now. It may not be pleasant, but the United States needs a thorough exam. Is America finally willing to let me grab its junk?

Hop up on the table. This may hurt a bit.

PART I

PREDISPOSED TO BEING UNHEALTHY

SURGEON GENERAL'S WARNING

"Black and Hispanic Americans are dying of the coronavirus disease at rates far higher than white Americans."

—*New York Times*, April 16, 2020

How could it be that we are to blame for our own deaths? Early in the pandemic, that's what we were being told.

The starkest example was when Trump's surgeon general, Jerome Adams, an African American doctor, held a press conference in April 2020, as the COVID crisis was just beginning to kill thousands of Americans. He got up there and blamed us for our own deaths. He said: "Avoid alcohol, tobacco, and drugs. . . . We need you to do this, if not for yourself, then for your abuela. Do it for your granddaddy. Do it for your Big Mama. Do it for your Pop-Pop.

We need you to understand—especially in communities of color, we need you to step up and help stop the spread so that we can protect those who are most vulnerable."

So why is he even mentioning "avoid alcohol, tobacco, and drugs"? Now how the fuck is a global pandemic gonna be our fault? But there he was, blaming us. Even before COVID hit here, it was killing people in Italy and Spain and China. I wonder: Did anybody at any point tell Italians that it was their fault? Or insinuate that it was Spanish people's fault? They got abuelas in Spain too, right? But in America, they made it seem as if it was our fault. The Trump administration sends out this young Black man to insinuate that it was our drinking and drug use and smoking that put us in this situation.

I mean, you can't tell me not to drink or do drugs or smoke and also to stay at home. It's gonna be one or the other. You know what I mean? I wanna be safe, but you're gonna have either a murderer or an alcoholic. You pick. At least if I'm an alcoholic, I get to leave the house to go to those twelve-step meetings. Whoever said "you're safer at home" never lived at my house.

Why is it Black and brown people who should stop

drinking? I know there are plenty of white drunks. We all gotta be in this together, right? Everybody better stop. Do it for your "Pop-Pop" and your "Big Mama"? Now, the surgeon general, who's a Black dude, defended himself when he was criticized, saying that he was just trying to "target" his message: "We need targeted outreach to the African American community, and I use the language that is used in my family. I have a Puerto Rican brother-in-law. I call my granddaddy 'Granddaddy.' I have relatives who call their grandparents 'Big Mama.'" But why is a Black man, working for a racist administration, "targeting" his own community's behavior in this way?

Here's what's funny about Jerome Adams. First off, I don't know how you get to be the fucking surgeon general and you're an anesthesiologist. Shouldn't you have to be a real doctor? Shouldn't the surgeon general be a surgeon or something? Oh, I forgot: Black surgeons are most qualified to run the Department of Housing and Urban Development, like Ben Carson.

However the fuck he got to be there, when he did his news conference, he was up there with his uniform *and* his inhaler. He's asthmatic. Like a lot of African Americans, he's had asthma since he was a kid. So, I'm sure he wasn't drinking or smoking as a kid. Black folks often grow up surrounded by factories, smokestacks, traffic pollution, and other unhealthy environments. But here he is, an asthmatic, blaming Black people for our health problems.

Adams, more than anyone, should know that if he's gonna stand up onstage with Trump and say stuff like this, he's not speaking to his community—he's toeing the line for an administration that blames us for all our problems.

WHAT THE HELL DO YOU HAVE TO LOSE?

"Hispanic and black Americans have been hardest hit in COVID-19 wage, job losses; most do not have rainy day funds."

—Pew Research Center

Remember when Trump was running in 2016 and he made his pitch to Black voters: "What do you have to lose? You're living in poverty. Your schools are no good. You have no jobs. Fifty-eight percent of your youth is unemployed. What the hell do you have to lose?"

And four years later, what have we lost? Welp, due to Trump's willful mishandling of the pandemic, we lost our jobs, we lost our homes, we lost our lives disproportionately. So: everything. We lost everything. We knew Trump was gonna be a disaster, but I don't think anyone could have predicted that this motherfucker would get so many people killed before we could vote him out. Even in my wildest imagination, I wouldn't have predicted it. If I told you at his inauguration that he'd have more people dead than in attendance, you'd think I was crazy

By the time Trump mercifully left office on January 20, 2021, more than four hundred thousand people had died of the coronavirus in the United States. And that's probably an undercount. It's the biggest failure of the Trump administration—perhaps of any presidency ever—a catastrophic toll that is unfathomable.

Trump's enablers didn't see it that way, of course. Throughout the pandemic, but especially early on, Fox News has worked hard to throw doubt at the numbers, downplay the virus's toll, and otherwise try to deny that their boy Trump fucked everything up.

Fox commentator Brit Hume, for example, tried to make

a distinction on Twitter between "those who die with the disease and those who die from it." Um, if you land in the hospital because of the virus, and then you die, you died *from* the virus. It doesn't matter if you also had diabetes or asthma; you wouldn't have died without the COVID. According to Hume and others, people with diabetes or asthma are partly to blame for their deaths. COVID was just their plus-one.

Then how about this? Trump's not the motherfucker who's to blame for four hundred thousand people dying of the coronavirus. He's the motherfucker who's to blame for four hundred thousand people dying, who *also* had the coronavirus. Does that work?

So maybe it's not easy to measure COVID deaths, especially because we had hardly any testing early on. Then isn't it more likely that we *underestimated* coronavirus deaths, not *overestimated* them? That's why experts measure "excess mortality." Excess mortality is the number of deaths in a health crisis like the COVID outbreak above what you would normally expect based on past years.

In New York City at the height of the outbreak, deaths were almost eight times higher than normal. Between

March and mid-August, the U.S. had more than 244,000 excess deaths, compared to 169,000 confirmed COVID-19 deaths during that period—a difference of 75,000 deaths. If that's not because of COVID, that's a lot of asthma.

THE EXPENDABLES

I firmly believe that the reason this disease has gotten out of control is because the majority of people dying early on were old, Black, brown, and poor. And we got a lot of them. America has a bountiful supply of old people, Black people, brown people, and poor people. Apparently they're expendable.

Because the coronavirus initially hit heavily Black and brown communities in places like Brooklyn, the Bronx, and San Francisco, it became easy for white people in red states to believe that it was mostly a "Black problem." Why mask up if no one you've ever met has died from the virus? When the problem's only happening to other people, when your president is refusing to wear a mask and downplaying the issue, doesn't it seem like there's something wrong with Black people?

Maybe it's biological? Maybe it's that Black people won't follow the rules? Maybe it's just an urban problem? In the early days, when it was just New York City or New Orleans getting hit, it was easy to be a white dude in the middle of nowhere who didn't know anyone with COVID.

According to data obtained by the *New York Times,* by May 2020 "Latino and African-American residents of the United States [were] three times as likely to become infected as their white neighbors, according to the new data, which provides detailed characteristics of 640,000 infections detected in nearly 1,000 U.S. counties. And Black and Latino people [were] nearly twice as likely to die from the virus as white people."

Three times as likely to catch the virus and twice as likely to die. That's stark.

And this was kinda early, before the surge brought the virus to the Midwest and the Southwest. Unfortunately for white folks, they didn't learn from what was happening. Maybe they thought white privilege extended to the pandemic and made them immune to COVID-19. But no, they just couldn't resist gathering in Sturgis, South Dakota, on their motorcycles to watch Smash Mouth. Or attending a party at the White House.

I DON'T WANT TO SEE YOUR FACE IN HERE

I never thought I would see America so frightened of a disease that they let niggas walk around with masks on. *"Hey you, get out of this bank with no mask on!"* I never thought I'd see that.

But not everyone got the memo. In America, a Black dude with a mask on is suspicious, even if the CDC told him to wear it. Masks might help us avoid catching the virus, but not catching a case for robbing a store.

In April 2020, Democratic Senators Cory Booker and Kamala Harris wrote a letter to attorney general Bill Barr and FBI director Christopher Wray requesting that they provide training and guidance to law enforcement agencies related to bias during the coronavirus outbreak after several racial incidents involving masks. They were basically saying, "Let the police departments know that niggas are gonna be wearing masks. A mask-wearing Black dude is not, in and of itself, suspicious."

In Wood River, Illinois, a couple of Black men were escorted out of a Walmart by a cop who told them their masks were illegal. In Miami, a Black doctor was handcuffed and detained by cops while wearing a mask as he unloaded a van in his front yard. The presumption of guilt makes it dangerous for Black men to wear masks at all. A state senator from Illinois was actually stopped after leaving his hardware store by a police officer who justified himself by saying, "I can't see your face. You look like you might have been up to something."

So even the prescriptions for us are dangerous. Even the things you're supposed to do to protect yourself, for us are dangerous. COVID-19 is deadly, but it doesn't kill you as fast as a suspicious cop. So some people have started wearing masks that look a little "safer." One guy on Twitter said, "I had the Bane mask. Forgot I'm Black. And big. And ancestrally red-eyed. And of the United States. New mask is floral. Don't shoot. Naw, for real. Don't shoot." Floral masks, something cute or silly—that protects you from coronavirus *and* from cops.

If you're shopping for masks, don't go looking for the same masks that white people are shopping for. Two-ply, N95 filters, adjustable straps—these aren't the considerations Black people need to worry about. A safe mask for white people might be a standard blue surgical mask, but if you're Black, the kind of blue mask you need is one that says "Blue Lives Matter," so they know you're not fucking with them. Maybe you want to wear a mask that seems homemade, but it's a lot safer for a Black dude to wear one that says "Make America Great Again." At least with these sorts of masks, your only injury is to your pride.

But there are lots of places in America where nobody wears masks. In red states where the government already doesn't give a shit about Black people, they barely put in any restrictions. Back before there was a vaccine in sight, with Republicans unwilling to buck President Trump, they decided it was okay for some niggers to die for their freedom to not wear masks.

They even tried to kill me! I mean, I know I piss some people off, but damn. You probably saw me fall off my stool at a club. I came from California, where there are mask mandates everywhere, and I went to Texas, where there weren't as many. And as a performer, I knew that if I wanted to perform, I had to go to a state where the government didn't give a fuck about its people. And that's how I got COVID. Lucky for me, I've made a full recovery.

But I think they missed their chance to get rid of me. Now there's literally so much plexiglass in a comedy club,

I don't know whether to tell a joke or fill my gas tank up. I'm in a bubble, with a plexiglass shield around me like I'm in a salad bar. Except no tongs, and I don't know who the tomatoes are: me or the audience.

WE GOTTA BE SOMEWHERE

It's not just stand-up comedians who are at risk. If you have to work and use public transportation, you're exposed in a different way than people working from home or driving their own cars are. If you're poor, living in an apartment with a lot of people, you're more likely to get infected. So all the ramifications of poverty and systemic racism make the virus more deadly to people of color.

According to census data from 2018, almost half of Black and Latino workers are employed in service or production jobs that you can't do from home. Only one in four white workers do similar work. These jobs are minimum-wage jobs, with bad working conditions.

In most counties with a large Black population, the infection rate was higher for Black residents than for white ones. The same was true for Latinos. So it's not just that certain regions weren't affected by the virus; the virus was hitting the same place but with different results for different people.

Early on, people kept talking about how the higher death rate among people of color was due to underlying health problems like diabetes. But if more Black and Latino people get the virus, the death rate is going to be higher. A white dude with diabetes who isn't exposed isn't going to get infected or die from the virus.

And if you don't have good health insurance, you're more likely to wait too long before getting medical care. These severe cases are more likely to result in death.

POSSIBLE SIDE EFFECTS OF NOT GIVING A FUCK

So it's not something wrong with Black people that's why we're dying in greater numbers. It's a side effect of America not giving a fuck about us. The biggest outbreaks have been among people who are treated badly, who don't have a choice.

COVID cases are higher among people who are being

warehoused: people in old-folks' homes, inmates, workers in meatpacking plants. They're warehoused in certain parts of town or nursing facilities or prisons. These people aren't to blame; they're *victims* of their circumstances.

Take prisoners. How can you blame inmates for getting infected if you control all of their circumstances? As of December 2020, at least 200,000 inmates had been infected with the coronavirus and at least 1,450 inmates and correctional officers had died, according to the *New York Times*. That's probably an undercount too, because they hardly test prisoners. Where they have tested, they found rampant spread; in Connecticut they tested 10,000 prisoners from March to June and found that 13 percent were infected. Testing in Texas found 26,000 infections, California had 18,000, and Florida had 17,000 as of December 2020. Who knows how many are really infected nationwide? What we do know is that prisons are full of people in tight quarters without any protection against the virus.

Despite this, authorities have been slow to act. At San Quentin State Prison in California, more than 2,200 people got sick and 28 died in the summer of 2020, but nothing was done. Even before the first death, an "Urgent Memo" from health experts stated that "San Quentin is an extremely dangerous place for an outbreak, everything should be done to decrease the number of people exposed to this environment as quickly as possible." In October, an appellate court told prison officials they had to release people to save their lives, requiring them to release 50 percent of their population.

We're talking about a population that is 40 percent Black. The only people white America cares less about than niggas are imprisoned niggas. These are people who, a lot of times, are already sick and susceptible to bad health. But America has written them off because they're "no angels." Well, most of the prisoners in the U.S. weren't given a death sentence until they were given COVID. The coronavirus doesn't need a nail file hidden in a cake to escape prison; coronavirus infects the prisoners and the guards and then their families and then their communities.

And Black people and Latinos are dying at higher rates because they're exposed at their low-paying jobs. Some of the biggest outbreaks have been in meatpacking plants. As of October 2020, more than a hundred meat-processing plants had outbreaks of COVID. More than forty-four thousand meatpacking workers had the virus and over two hundred workers had died.

At a Tyson Foods plant in Waterloo, Iowa, more than one thousand workers contracted the virus and at least five died. The family of one of the workers filed a wrongful death lawsuit that detailed horrible working conditions. Employees allegedly were told they had to report to work while sick, in cramped conditions, and without protective gear.

When the local sheriff visited the plant, he said what he saw "shook me to the core," according to an interview with the *New York Times*. Many of them were immigrants, working elbow to elbow with no face masks. The sheriff tried to get Tyson to shut the plant down, but they wouldn't.

Managers told supervisors to ignore symptoms and ordered an employee who vomited on the production line to keep working. According to the complaint in the wrongful death lawsuit, one manager said that it was a "glorified flu" and told workers not to worry about getting it. When more employees on the production floor started showing symptoms, managers wouldn't go to the plant floor. But plant supervisors denied that there were any cases and paid workers bonuses to keep working while sick. Not only that, the complaint alleged, the plant manager created a betting pool for supervisors and managers on how many employees would test positive. They were betting on these people's lives.

And why was it so important for these workers to risk their lives? Trump ordered it. He used the Defense Production Act to order meat and poultry processing companies to stay open and keep working. Do Americans need hot dogs so bad that they want to kill people over it? I don't remember the chicken sandwich that I'd murder a motherfucker for. I'd eat some tofu if it meant that a worker could go home to his family.

Trump didn't use the Defense Production Act to ramp up production of ventilators or order up personal protective equipment (PPE) for hospital workers. He used it to make sure that people could keep eating Big Macs. Except that actually, that's not what happened. Because instead of feeding Americans, these meat companies sold most of their products to China. In April, while Tyson Foods warned that "millions of pounds of meat will disappear" from supply chains if Trump didn't act, they actually sold more pork to China than they had since January 2017. Smith-field Foods, another large food-processing company, had one of its highest monthly export totals of the last three years. According to research compiled by Panjiva and the U.S. Department of Agriculture, a record 129,000 tons of pork were exported to China. I hope they enjoyed the hell out of their mu shu pork.

And the other outbreaks were in nursing homes. Unfortunately, our elders don't always have the best people working for them. Let me rephrase that: These facilities don't pay their employees enough to give a fuck about old people. Even a 2020 Health and Human Services report backs me up: "Nursing homes pay large proportions of NAs [nursing assistants] at the minimum wage, resulting in challenges associated with recruiting and retaining employees, which may in turn decrease care quality and reduce access to LTC [long-term care] services." People in nursing homes are in close proximity to each other, and cared for at the lowest cost possible. Society has put them aside.

Minimum-wage employees at meatpacking plants, grocery stores, and nursing homes aren't heroes. They've never been "essential workers" or they would've been paid to be "essential." Black and brown people are dying from this so that you can live.

If you're an old white person in a nursing home, you're more likely to die because society hasn't cared enough to make sure you live. White people can actually live so long that they get treated like niggas. I bet some of the old racists dying in a nursing home couldn't fucking believe that that's how they ended up being treated. It's crazy. You can live your whole life to become a nigga.

SPANISH FLU II

America didn't just start not giving a fuck about Black people. This might be a novel coronavirus, but the situation isn't novel. This unprecedented health crisis has precedent.

If you look at the last big pandemic, the Spanish flu of 1918, Black people were dying the same way then as they are today with the coronavirus. It's eerie how similar it was to now. Twenty million to fifty million people died around the world, including 675,000 Americans. Back then, conditions were even worse for poor people, things were even more segregated, and there was little to no medical treatment available to Black people. There were no vaccines and nobody knew how to treat the Spanish flu, anyway. And of course, people didn't want to wear masks then either.

And just like today, there were superspreader events. Even though Trump knew that coronavirus could be transmitted through the air back in February 2020, events like the Mardi Gras parade in New Orleans went on anyway because local officials didn't have that information. Nobody from the CDC warned the mayor of New Orleans or the governor of Louisiana to consider canceling the parade, and as a result, it spread COVID all over the city and the surrounding areas. It was the same in 1918, when the mayor of Philadelphia let a parade go forward despite a Spanish flu outbreak; within ten days, thousands of people were dead. When Trump said that the coronavirus was just like a normal flu, he was saying the same stuff that got people killed back in Philadelphia. Back then, even though nearby army bases were already having a deadly outbreak of the Spanish flu, the city's public health director, Wilmer Krusen, said that it was only "old-fashioned influenza or grip."

And just like now, the president got sick. In 1919,

Woodrow Wilson caught the Spanish flu on his way to Paris for peace talks. He tried to hide his illness and downplay its severity. He told the press that he was just overworked and that the cold Paris weather had given him a cold. In fact, he couldn't sit up in bed; he had coughing fits and a 103-degree fever. Wilson was so sick that he started blurting out unexpected orders and he became convinced that he was surrounded by French spies. Luckily, he didn't have Twitter, so he couldn't tweet-storm like Trump: *LIL KAISER WILHELM MUST ACCEPT TERMS OF THE BIG FOUR!*

Wilson didn't want to talk about the flu outbreak, and he never expressed public regrets for his handling of the epidemic. Back then they didn't track medical data like we do today, so it's hard to get an accurate count of how many Black people died of the Spanish flu. The conventional "wisdom" at the time was that Black people were dying of the disease at lower rates than white people. This could have been due to underreporting or it might have been that segregation created a kind of quarantine. It might also have been that the Black population had previous exposure to a weaker version of the flu. Scholars disagree.

But everybody agrees that because of segregation and

poverty, Black people were forced to live in the dirtiest parts of town with the fewest resources available. As an example, in Baltimore, even prior to the flu, the Biddle Alley tenement slum area had a block known as a "lung block" because there was so much tuberculosis there. Then this level of sickness was used against Black people as a further justification for segregation and withholding resources. With barely any hospitals that served Black people, flu patients had to quarantine at home, where there was no treatment available. Even in Black hospitals like the Frederick Douglass Memorial Hospital in Philadelphia, all seventy-five beds were filled with flu victims, and they had to open an annex in a school nearby.

This scarcity of resources is the same thing we faced in the early weeks and months of the pandemic when there was no treatment and no help from the federal government. The vast majority of people at the public hospitals in New York City when COVID first hit were people of color. According to the *New York Times,* at the peak of the outbreak there in April 2020, patients in New York's community hospitals were three times more likely to die than patients at New York's well-funded private medical facilities. Community hospitals didn't have enough staff or equipment. They were deprived of PPE and didn't have access to drug trials.

Nobody wants to criticize hospitals trying to do their best with limited resources, but underfunding hospitals is a choice that America makes. It's just another way that racism punishes Black and brown people by depriving them of the care white people routinely get. The *Times* spotlighted how two hospitals within a block of each other differed in their care. On the one hand was the well-funded NYU Langone Health, with a coronavirus mortality rate of about 11 percent as of July 2020. On the other hand, we had Bellevue Hospital Center, with a coronavirus mortality rate of double that: 22 percent. Some hospitals were even worse; at the Coney Island Hospital, 41 percent of coronavirus patients had died. Is it surprising that Coney Island Hospital serves poor people and people of color? Why is this acceptable in America?

In 1918, the *Chicago Defender*, one of the major Black newspapers, called on the police to stop warehousing prisoners in unsanitary conditions to help slow the spread of the pandemic: "The Chicago police stations are doing more to breed disease than any other agency supposed to be working for good in the city of Chicago. The methods used in various stations of huddling numbers of prisoners together, holding them sometimes thirty-six hours without any medical examination . . . is of itself a breeder of disease, and represents the uncivilized and barbaric age." And still, here we are in 2020 with the police locking up protesters in confined spaces at police stations. What's changed in the prisons of 2020, where wardens denied basic protective gear to prisoners?

So there's been a long history of America not caring about Black and brown people. Again and again, when it's people of color being hurt, it's not important to act; after all, we're different, right? We're not as human, not worth the same protections as white people. If freeing prisoners, or closing meatpacking plants, or providing the same PPE to Black people could save lives, why aren't you doing it?

And even though we knew that basically if everyone just stayed home for a while, we could save a lot of lives, Trump's attorney general Bill Barr was critical of the idea of a national lockdown. He said, "Other than slavery . . . this is the greatest intrusion on civil liberties in American history."

Because white people are so devoid of actual persecution, they always gotta pretend that shit done to them is "like slavery." They have to co-opt Black people's oppression. Staying home ain't slavery. Wearing a mask ain't slavery. Nah. You didn't ship me and the motherfuckers from Africa across the mid-Atlantic to wear masks. Motherfucker, you don't have monuments to people who wore masks. What the fuck are you talking about?

And instead of blaming white people for *actually* killing people by not staying home, Bill Barr made them sound like defenders of freedom. *Don't you see? The real villains are Black people drinking too much and the real heroes are Trump supporters coughing on each other at a motorcycle rally, singing "Hey now, you're an all-star . . ."*

PART II

AMERICA HAS PREEXISTING CONDITIONS

If Black people have suffered more in this outbreak, it's because America has set it up that way. America has preexisting conditions on health: if you're Black, you're more likely to die. It's been that way since we were brought here as slaves, and the legacy of slavery is still impacting us today.

BUT THE BIBLE SAYS

Tom Cotton, Republican senator from Arkansas, doesn't think that slavery is America's original sin. He proposed a law, the Saving American History Act, that would penalize schools for using the *New York Times*'s 1619 Project curriculum in their history courses. This Pulitzer Prize–winning series traced the reality of slavery in America back to 1619, the date the first enslaved African arrived in Virginia (that's about three hundred years before the first Trumps arrived, by the way), and argued that an understanding of slavery and the contributions of Black Americans should be "at the very center of our national narrative." Well, this ruffled Senator Cotton's feathers. He said, "The 1619 Project is left-wing propaganda. It's revisionist history at its worst. . . . The entire premise of the *New York Times*'s factually, historically flawed 1619 Project . . . is that America is, at root, a systemically racist country to the core and irredeemable." He added, "As the Founding Fathers said, it was the necessary evil upon which the Union was built."

As much as people like Tom Cotton try to downplay slavery's role in the foundation of our country, the fact of the matter is that the enslavement of Black people could only happen if we were viewed from the get-go as subhuman and culpable in our own ruin. And that history of slavery infected America and remains the source of systemic racism in our society to this day. You see, Black people were viewed as biologically different from the start. We gotta be different so it's okay to treat us different.

But white people didn't just make this shit up! It was in *the Bible.* So, you know, God told them it was okay. Christianity, in early America, was proslavery. The Bible was used to justify slavery because, according to some, Africans were the cursed descendants of Ham. I know, it surprises me that there's Ham in the Bible too, because all you ever hear about is bread and wine. Add a little cheese, you got the beginnings of a sandwich. But I digress.

In the book of Genesis, right after the Great Flood, Noah gets drunk on some wine and passes out naked in his tent. One of his sons, Ham, stumbles upon his dad in all his glory and tells his brothers, Shem and Japheth. And let me just say, for all the shit white people give us about us naming our kids "Kiara" or "Malik," how come we never hear anything about "Ham," "Shem," and "Japheth?" Look, I know the Bible was written by Middle Eastern dudes, but you've got to admit the irony of these Bible-thumpers in the "Christian Right." They'll throw DeAndre's résumé in the trash, but the book about Shem and Ham is the word of God?

In any case, Shem and Japheth don't want to see their dad naked, so instead of pointing and laughing like Ham did, they cover him up. And when Noah wakes up, he's pissed. He curses Ham and says "'Cursed be Canaan! The lowest of slaves will he be to his brothers.'" Right there, you have a white dude blaming us for shit that ain't our fault.

So Ham and his descendants are cursed to be slaves for all time because Noah couldn't hold his liquor. I guess anyone who could have cut him off had been washed away in the flood. Now, how did Black people come to be the descendants of Ham? The logic is a bit circular, but of course, because Black people were slaves, they must be descendants of Ham, and thus the Bible says they should be slaves forever. It's kind of a chicken/egg problem. Or a Ham/egg problem, maybe.

Later on in the Bible, God tells Moses a million little instructions on how to live. Slaveholders in the 1800s liked to quote Leviticus 25:44–46: "Your male and female slaves are to come from the nations around you; from them you may buy slaves. You may also buy some of the temporary residents living among you and members of their clans born in your country, and they will become your property. You can bequeath them to your children as inherited property and can make them slaves for life, but you must not rule over your fellow Israelites ruthlessly." This was taken as justification for slavery, because God was cool with slaves back then, so why wouldn't he be cool now? But God also told Moses, "Anyone who sells a house in a walled city retains the right of redemption a full year after its sale. During that time the seller may redeem it. If it is not redeemed before a full year has passed, the house in the walled city shall belong permanently to the buyer and the buyer's descendants. It is not to be returned in the Jubilee." So this micromanager God had a lot of little rules that nobody was paying much attention to by 1830, right? I mean, people weren't going around worrying about their houses in walled cities, but they were worried about their slaves.

People even pointed out that Jesus never said shit about slavery, so it must be okay. I guess the thinking was that Jesus was supposed to be such a great dude, and he had so much to say, he would've said something about slavery if it were a problem. Jesus also never said anything about ham sandwiches, but I don't think that means he was pro–ham sandwich. Sorry I keep talking about ham sandwiches, I must be hungry.

Once it's okay by God and Jesus to have slavery, then maybe slavery is even a *good* thing, right? I mean, how else are all these Africans going to get into heaven if we don't capture them, force them to work, rape them, and separate them from their families *but also* tell them about Jesus?

Then we can tell them how important it is to be obedient, good servants and so on.

As Black people learned the Bible, of course, they started to reject these notions. And the Black church in America has been a powerful force in the civil rights movement and toward racial justice. But the split between white and Black Christians in America is still here. Church in America is still totally segregated; as of 2014, 80 percent of churchgoers in America went to churches where at least 80 percent of the congregation is of only one race. So while Black churches have focused on civil rights, white churches have not. White churchgoers no longer believe that the Bible justifies slavery, obviously, but white evangelicals were among the strongest supporters of Trump. Instead of working toward racial justice, evangelicals focus on criminalizing abortion.

It's interesting to me that Black people and white people can look at the same Bible and come to different conclusions. The justification of slavery in the Bible, the formation of the Black and white churches, and their continued segregation to this day perpetuates racism. Bishop Claude Alexander of the Park Church in Charlotte, North Carolina, told the *Washington Post,* "The church gave spiritual sanction [to racism], both overtly by the things that it taught and covertly by the critique that it did not raise." His theory on why Black and white churches have different political priorities? "If I've never experienced oppression or marginalization outside of the womb, then it's easy for me to make what happens inside the womb a priority."

WEIRD SCIENCE

I hope we can agree that the Bible is not a reliable source of information. If it were, we'd all still think the Earth was flat. So once "scientists" started looking around for another reason it was okay to enslave Black people, they came up with "scientific" justifications for their white supremacy. *Why are there Black people? Why are there white people? Why is it so much better to be white than Black?*

Maybe Black skin was caused by the heat of Africa? Bear in mind, this was long before Darwin and our understanding of genetics. Or maybe it had to do with the humors of the body? You know, the humors—not *ha ha* humors, the "four humors": blood, yellow bile, black bile, and phlegm. Maybe Black people had an imbalance of the humors. That was once the main theory of why people got sick: their humors were imbalanced. (That's why I called it "science.")

I know. It sounds crazy. Imbalanced humors sounds like watching somebody fall over, which is always hilarious. Except when I fell off my stool in Nashville and found out I had COVID. That shit was not funny at all.

But after a while, they settled on a theory that Africans had *devolved* from white people. By a process of "degeneration," Black people and others had been created through perversions and deterioration. So it was basically the opposite of what the fossil record shows; instead of Black people leaving Africa and becoming racist *white* people, they thought *white* people went to Africa and got so hot that they became dope Black people. And then white people who had stayed home went and captured those Black people.

In fact, the term "Caucasian" comes from Johann Friedrich Blumenbach's theory that the original people (white, of course) came from the Caucasus region. You know, where Noah's ark landed. Because science. Blumenbach studied his large collection of skulls and tried to explain differences in skin color by classifying everyone into three "races": Caucasoid, Mongoloid, and Negroid.

Back in America, another big skull collector, Samuel Morton, became influential for his theory that the different races were actually different *species,* with a natural hicrarchy. I'm gonna let you guess which race he thought was on the top. You see, Morton thought that it was impossible to have the variety of races in the world all stemming from just the three sons of Noah. By pouring grains of rice into the cavities of skulls, he was able to measure the inside volume and thus, the brain capacity. Naturally, the bigger the brain, the bigger the intellect.

With these measurements in hand, he posited that (okay, I'll tell you) Caucasians had the biggest brains, Native Americans had smaller brains, and Black people had the smallest. Since he had a bunch of skulls from Egypt that didn't fit his idea, he decided that Egyptians must have been Caucasians too. When he published these ideas in the 1830s and 1840s, they were used as "scientific justification" for the enslavement of Black people. The inherent differences between races clearly caused the white race to be "distinguished for the facility with which it attains the highest intellectual endowments" and Black people to be "joyous, flexible, and indolent; while the many nations which compose this race present a singular diversity of intellectual character, of which the far extreme is the lowest grade of humanity." You know what? I do feel joyous and flexible sometimes, but it usually has less to do with the size of my skull and more to do with the size of my drink.

It might be easy to laugh off these antiquated notions about the biological differences between the races, if it weren't for the fact that these biases still affect Black and brown people in America today. You see it in health outcomes. You see it in the way doctors treat us. You heard it in Trump's racist words and policies—and still do among his followers in congress.

We don't have enough pages in the book to list all of Trump's racist language and actions, but this attitude of white supremacy is inherent in him saying about Mexican immigrants, "These aren't people. These are animals." And his policies reinforced that.

AMERICAN BREEDERS

Because, look: If Black and brown people are predisposed to violence and disease, if we're subhuman, why not use medical science to eliminate the problem? Eugenics was an American specialty. If that shit sounds a lot like Nazi Germany, that's because the Nazis basically learned their moves from America. Hitler himself praised America's eugenics program in *Mein Kampf.*

Nowadays, you can't go around saying you're into eugenics without sounding like you're a Nazi. Hitler sort of ruined eugenics for most people. I mean, Hitler ruined a lot of stuff for a lot of people. You hardly ever see tiny mustaches anymore, for example. Or *Heil Hitler* salutes, at least until the Trump years. Eugenics and "race purity"? Most people sort of moved on.

But in the early twentieth century, eugenics gained a lot of traction in America. By encouraging "superior" people to reproduce and discouraging those with "undesirable" characteristics from doing so, fans of eugenics thought it was possible to create a better human race. And of course, white people were the ones who got to decide what was desirable and what wasn't.

This wasn't some fringe theory just for mad scientists. Prominent people signed on to this idea. In 1911, John Harvey Kellogg, inventor of Kellogg's cereal, also founded the Race Betterment Foundation. It worked on eugenics policies, such as the forced sterilization of "mentally defective people" and opposition to "racial mixing." White people: *They're gr-r-reat!*

But yeah, Kellogg was a weird dude. He also headed up an anti-masturbation movement, which is surprising from the guy who created Frosted Flakes.

In a number of states, policies were put into place to basically try to breed Black people out. If you're inclined to blame Black people and poor people for longstanding social problems, then of course it makes sense to make sure that they can't reproduce. It was just another way in which white people sought to control Black people's bodies. Back in the days of slavery, slave owners sought to make sure their slaves had large families so they'd have a lot of little children to enslave. And now, the white establishment sought to ensure that Black people had no children. But the white supremacist mentality was the same.

Literally at the same time Josef Mengele was doing what he was doing, America was doing what it was doing. Everyone agrees that what the Nazis did was a hideous war crime. But not many people know the extent of forced sterilizations here in America. Thirty-three different states enacted sterilization laws.

Virginia carried out the second-most sterilizations, with about eight thousand. Virginia's law was appealed to the Supreme Court, where the court ruled *against* Carrie Buck, a young woman who had been raped at age seventeen and then had a child out of wedlock, after which Virginia forced her to be sterilized. Justice Oliver Wendell Holmes Jr.'s opinion read, in part: "It is better for all the world, if instead of waiting to execute degenerate offspring for crime or to let them starve for their imbecility, society can prevent those who are manifestly unfit from continuing their kind. . . . Three generations of imbeciles are enough." *Three Generations of Imbeciles Are Enough* sounds like a Trump family biography, but I digress.

Even after most states stopped their eugenics programs after World War II, North Carolina expanded theirs. More than 7,600 people were sterilized under their program. The Eugenics Board of North Carolina held hearings that often lasted only a few minutes. Despite the pleas of many who appeared before the panel, the verdict was almost always sterilization. A group of wealthy businessmen in Winston-Salem formed the Human Betterment League of North Carolina in 1947 to promote the program, and it actually gained massive public support. This group included

Dr. Clarence Gamble, an heir to the Procter & Gamble fortune, and James G. Hanes of Hanes underwear fame. When you're sterilizing women, that's not "Hanes Her Way," that's Hanes your way.

I mean, think about that: After World War II, after the Nazis, the rich people of North Carolina still pushed for an expansion of the sterilization of poor people, Black people, and the mentally ill. They made their pitch in newspaper editorials, at luncheons, and in pamphlets. Sterilization was presented as a cure-all for many problems such as a diluted white gene pool and a growing population of "defectives."

But by the 1960s, the argument for sterilization had moved from protecting the gene pool to protecting the wallet. According to an investigation by the *Winston-Salem Journal*, by the late 1960s more than 60 percent of those sterilized were Black and 99 percent were women. In an interview with the *Journal*, Dr. A. M. Stanton, one of the doctors who performed sterilizations, said that sterilization "was probably a good thing. . . . I think some people did it on purpose (had children) to get a little bit of extra money from the welfare department." Social workers told Black women that they would lose their welfare if they didn't get sterilized. This argument against "welfare queens," as Reagan would later name them, was used to continue a program that targeted Black women. With no training and little oversight, social workers could recommend sterilization for anyone they wanted.

North Carolina's program lasted until 1974. Let that sink in: 1974. Kool & the Gang were singing "Jungle Boogie" and North Carolina was sterilizing poor Black women.

Finally, in 2010, the governor of North Carolina established a fund to compensate victims who were forcibly sterilized with a $50,000 payment. Even today, some people are still waiting to get their money as they appeal denials and seek their full amounts. So this history is still with us today. We're not talking about a long time ago.

The biggest sterilization program was in California, with over twenty-one thousand victims between 1909 and 1979. They kicked it off with the "Asexualization Act" of 1909. Most of the sterilizations happened prior to 1950, but the laws weren't revoked until 1979, when several working-class Mexican women sued after having been coerced into tubal ligations after having cesarian births. And like elsewhere, this program was initially justified as a way to apply science to "social problems." Asylums and prisons were authorized to "asexualize" patients or inmates. "Hereditary insanity" was one justification, along with "various grades of feeblemindedness" and so on. This was all framed as a benefit to the public, but of course it was racist as hell. Thank God they stopped before we got Kanye.

Later, ideas about population control and racist fears of welfare fraud were used to perpetuate abuse like this.

In 1973, two Black sisters, Minnie Lee Relf and Mary Alice Relf, brought a lawsuit with the help of the Southern Poverty Law Center for having been sterilized without their consent at the ages of twelve and fourteen, respectively. The two sisters had been taken to a doctor's office and told they were getting "birth control shots." Their mother, who went with them, couldn't read or write. She signed "X" on the consent form they were given. This case brought to light a number of other examples of Black and Native American women being forcibly sterilized. The federal judge in the Relfs' case, Judge Gerhard Gesell, concluded that "an indefinite number of poor people have been improperly coerced into accepting a sterilization operation under the threat that various federally supported welfare benefits would be withdrawn unless they submitted to irreversible sterilization. Patients receiving Medicaid assistance at childbirth are evidently the most frequent targets of this pressure."

It wasn't just forced sterilizations. The practice of performing hysterectomies without consent was widespread in many parts of the country throughout the 1960s and 1970s. Civil rights activist Fannie Lou Hamer told the story of having her uterus removed while in the hospital for a minor surgery in 1961. Southern doctors often used a visit to the hospital as a pretense for performing a hysterectomy; this happened so regularly that the procedure was nicknamed a "Mississippi appendectomy."

So Black people in America come by their fear of doctors honestly. The medical establishment has also used Black people as test subjects throughout America's history, but you don't have to go all the way back to slavery to find examples.

In 1932, the U.S. Public Health Service, along with the Tuskegee Institute, started a study of syphilis called the

"Tuskegee Study of Untreated Syphilis in the Negro Male."
I mean, fuck: Do you think anyone would knowingly sign
up for a study called "The Study of *Untreated* Syphilis"? Six
hundred Black men were put into the study and told that
they would get free medical exams, meals, and burial insurance in exchange for treatment of "bad blood." Most of
these men were poor sharecroppers who had never received
medical treatment before. Among the subjects, 399 had
syphilis and 201 did not. But none of them was actually
treated. Doctors lied to the men and gave them all placebos
instead of anything that might help with syphilis. Even after penicillin was shown to help treat the disease in 1947,
researchers convinced local doctors not to treat the men.

In the midsixties, a Public Health Service investigator,
Peter Buxtun, found out about the study and tried to get
it shut down. But officials decided to continue the study
anyway. So Buxtun leaked the story to the press in 1972
and public outrage forced it to stop. By that point, 28 of the
men had died of syphilis, another 100 had died from related complications, 40 of their spouses had also contracted
the disease, and 19 of their children were born with it.

We're not talking about a long time ago: 1972. And this

study was only stopped because of a whistleblower leaking to the press. Otherwise, maybe it would've lasted until 2004, when the final participant died. In 1973, Congress held hearings on the study and enacted new ethical reforms. A class-action lawsuit filed by the participants was settled with a $9 million payout, but the damage caused by the study extended beyond the people who were directly involved.

A paper published in 2016 by Marcella Alsan at the Stanford University School of Medicine and Marianne Wanamaker at the University of Tennessee estimated that the mistrust bred by the Tuskegee Experiment actually reduced life expectancy among Black men over forty-five by more than a year. This makes sense because whenever you talk to Black men about why they don't want to go to the doctor, they bring up the Tuskegee Experiment. If you were around for the hearings or the apology President Bill Clinton gave in 1997, or if you just know our history, it sits in our psyche as something doctors might do to us. How can Black people trust doctors in America after something like that?

And a lot of the biological research that is done today

would not be possible if not for a Black woman whose cells were harvested without her knowledge or permission. Henrietta Lacks was a Black woman who underwent treatment at the Johns Hopkins Hospital in Baltimore in 1951 for abdominal pain. She was found to have an aggressive cervical cancer that killed her within the year. But while she was at the hospital, samples of her cancerous cells were sent to a researcher. These cells turned out to be able to reproduce at a very high rate and could live for an unusually long time. This cell line was harvested and duplicated in the lab to create the "HeLa" line that is used widely in medical research to this day.

All this would have been totally unknown to the public, except that when some of the cells were contaminated in the 1970s, researchers contacted the Lacks family for more samples. It wasn't until 1975 that Henrietta's relatives learned that her cells were still being used for treatments and research. None of the companies that used her cells has ever paid the family or shared with them the profits generated from her contribution. In 2010, Rebecca Skloot, the author of *The Immortal Life of Henrietta Lacks,* created the Henrietta Lacks Foundation, which provides assistance to families that have been impacted by medical research done without consent, and Oprah made a movie of the book. Only now are labs starting to grapple with their obligations to the legacy of using Henrietta Lacks's genetic material without her consent.

Accountability for past medical abuse has been slow to come. Until recently, New York City's Central Park had a statue to J. Marion Sims, the "father of modern gynecology," who experimented on enslaved women without anesthesia. The statue was put up in 1934 and removed only in 2018. Some of the defenders of Sims's reputation have noted that anesthesia wasn't commonly used at that time. But the reason he didn't use it was because the women were essentially leased out to Sims for his experiments. "I made this proposition to the owners of the negroes: If you will give me Anarcha and Betsey for experiment, I agree to perform no experiment or operation on either of them to endanger their lives, and will not charge a cent for keeping them, but you must pay their taxes and clothe them," he wrote in his autobiography. He operated on ten different women, one of them at least thirty times.

Regardless of Sims's achievements, these women had no

opportunity to withhold consent. If you don't see Black and brown people as fully human, you can do lots of things to them.

And America is still doing it.

In September 2020, a nurse filed a whistleblower complaint alleging medical neglect and abuse against detained immigrants in an ICE detention center, including unsanitary conditions and a refusal to test for coronavirus. According to the complaint, immigrants were detained in filthy facilities and denied required medications. One woman said she was denied breast cancer medication for six weeks. People who spoke up were punished with solitary confinement.

And an alarming number of women were sent to a doctor and given hysterectomies. The whistleblower said, "Everybody he sees has a hysterectomy—just about everybody . . . That's his specialty, he's the uterus collector. I know that's ugly . . . is he collecting these things or something . . . Everybody he sees, he's taking all their uteruses out or he's taken their tubes out." The Daily Beast reported that this doctor wasn't even a certified gynecologist.

Maybe that sounds hard to believe. *The Uterus Collector—*

that sounds like a low-budget horror movie. But our nation's history is rife with examples of abuse like this. We've done all kinds of evil shit to people of color under the auspices of doing science. This is par for the course.

UNNECESSARY SURGERY

So, of course it's outrageous that immigrants are being given unnecessary hysterectomies. But virtually the same thing is happening to Black women all the time. One may be for political purposes and the other for profit, but they're similar in that they're both being done to people who often don't have great doctors or adequate health insurance. They're not gonna really get a second opinion.

And it's pretty insidious: hysterectomy is one of the most commonly performed surgeries on women in America, and it's primarily done on Black women.

It could be that fibroids are to blame for some of this difference, because Black women are two to three times more likely than white women to have these growths and they tend to be larger. Uterine fibroids are common noncancerous tumors that develop in the womb. Fibroids can cause pelvic pain and severe bleeding that can interfere with women's lives in multiple ways. Women might miss work, be unable to do physical activities, and have other problems.

Now, why do Black women get more fibroids? One theory is that they're having sex with demons in their dreams. At least that's the cause proposed by Dr. Stella Immanuel, one of Donald Trump's favorite doctors. She's the one who came out on the steps of the Supreme Court to say that hydroxychloroquine cures COVID and that you don't need to wear a mask. First off, if there actually was a cure for COVID, they would never let a Black person be the first one to tell you. They don't let niggas give good news. Second, just 'cause she's got a white lab coat on, that doesn't make her an expert on COVID or fibroids or any other thing. Immanuel is a pediatrician and minister from Africa, now based in Houston. In one of her many online sermons, she says that fibroids are caused by demon sperm left by evil spirits.

Actually, fibroids for Black women have been linked to chemicals in their hair. In a study of twenty-three thousand women, researchers found a correlation between Black girls' use of straightening and relaxer hair oils and the risk of developing fibroids. Black women spend billions of dollars on their hair, and who knows what some of these chemicals do? So maybe it's demons and maybe it's chemical exposure. If it's a demon, it's called Dark and Lovely. Hell, that's a pretty good name for a demon, actually.

The difference in hysterectomy rates between Black women and non-Black women is likely because of differences in patient education and the doctors involved. Most hysterectomies are done to remove benign tumors, and even though they are the most effective treatment for fibroids, they also make it impossible for the women to get pregnant.

Black people have worse health outcomes in America for a host of reasons. But one big one is that we have way less access to care than white people do. How can we stay as healthy as y'all if we can't go to the doctor?

Obamacare brought insurance to people of color at an incredible rate. Before the Affordable Care Act, one in five Black people didn't have insurance, compared to one in eight white people. The biggest increases in coverage were for Black people, but they could have been even bigger if the states run by Republicans had approved Medicaid expansions. How can you separate out racism when more than 90 percent of the people who didn't get coverage are in the South? Given history, how can you call it anything else when Alabama, Florida, Georgia, Kansas, Mississippi, Missouri, North Carolina, Oklahoma, South Carolina, Tennessee, and Texas didn't approve coverage? These are the states with the largest Black populations, mostly run by Republican governors and legislatures. If they had approved the Medicaid expansion, 15 million more Black people would have health insurance.

NOT ENOUGH SHITTY CARE

Black people have less insurance, and even when we go to the doctor, the care is worse. The 2018 National Healthcare Quality and Disparities Report shows that we have worse care than white people, especially when it comes to timely access to care: we're twice as likely to have difficulties getting treatment when needed. A report by the National Academy of Medicine found that "racial and ethnic minorities receive lower-quality health care than white people—even when insurance status, income, age, and severity of conditions are comparable." What that means in practice is that we're given less attention, less pain meds, and older treatments. We're less likely to get bypass operations when we have heart disease, more likely to be discharged from the hospital earlier, and more likely to have our legs amputated for treatable diabetes. What's the point of going home early if you're gonna have a heart attack before you can relax and put your foot up?

So the quality of our health care is worse and we have less of it. It's like that old joke: "The food was terrible—and the portions were too small." We get shitty care, and not enough of it.

Here's just a few stark stats:

- Black men die of prostate cancer at two and a half times the rate of white men.
- Black men die of AIDS at six times the rate of white men.
- Black women are three times more likely to die from childbirth than white women.
- Black babies are expected to live three fewer years than white babies.
- Black babies are twice as likely to die before their first birthday as white babies.

WE DON'T TRUST YOU

It makes me so angry to think that from the very first moment, Black babies have less of a chance of living than white babies. Right from the beginning, we die more.

Childbirth is already a very precarious time for anyone, but for Black babies it's even deadlier if they have a white doctor. A study by George Mason University found that when cared for by white doctors, Black babies are three times more likely to die than white babies. But it reverses the other way if you have Black doctors and nurses; the mortality rate shrank up to 58 percent when a Black doctor was in charge.

I'm gonna be a grandfather soon. It's my first grandbaby. One night my daughter called me crying because her doctor wasn't listening to her about how she felt. And every pregnant woman worries about her pregnancy and doesn't want her feelings to be dismissed. You know, every woman feels as if there's never been another person pregnant ever on earth. Each person's birth is special, rightfully so, that's how they experience it. But she didn't like how her doctor was treating her. And she's married to a doctor, so I guess she normally likes doctors okay. Finally they decided to go to another doctor and now she feels better. But she knew to advocate for herself in a way that a lot of Black women don't feel comfortable doing.

That gut feeling we have with some doctors is telling us something. The same implicit bias that colors all our interactions with white people exists in health care as well. Multiple studies have shown that doctors are not immune to the biases that exist in society more generally. The difference is that if the dude at the gas station counter gives you the evil eye, it's less deadly than if your heart doctor won't prescribe you the meds you need. You might get the stink eye, but you're not a dead guy.

Implicit bias affects doctor-patient interactions, treatment decisions, and thus outcomes. This is regardless of income or access to care. So your doctor isn't gonna call you a "nigger," but he still might treat you like one. Studies show that doctors spend more time with white patients and keep Black patients waiting longer. When we do get in to see the doctor, we're more likely to get treated in a condescending manner and not have our opinions listened to.

If you go into the doctor's office and he never lets you

talk, that might be implicit bias at work. Researchers showed that doctors who scored high on implicit bias tests were more likely to commandeer most of the time spent with patients, and were most likely to do so with Black patients.

And we can tell. Black patients consistently rank high-implicit-bias doctors lower and are less confident in those doctors' opinions.

The story of Dr. Susan Moore, a Black physician, epitomizes the very struggle we're talking about. Dr. Moore entered a hospital outside of Indianapolis for treatment for COVID-19 and was denied proper care. She had to beg for remdesivir, the same experimental treatment that Donald Trump was given. Then, after experiencing severe pain, she was denied pain medication because her doctor said, "I don't feel comfortable giving you any more narcotics." As a doctor herself, Moore understood that her treatment wasn't adequate and she posted a video to Facebook about her experience. In the video, she said, "He made me feel like I was a drug addict. And he knew I was a physician. . . . You have to show proof that you have something wrong with you in order for you to get the medicine. I put forward and I maintain that if I was white, I wouldn't have to go through that."

This woman basically predicted her own death. After being prematurely discharged, she ended up back in the hospital and reliant on a ventilator to breathe. She was intubated and died several days later.

This sort of thing plays out all over the country, in all kinds of ways, every single day. There was generally no outrage. It wasn't like the George Floyd video. It was just kind of a benign acceptance of the way it is. There was no call to action, there was no movement started, there was just a resignation that it was an all-too-familiar story. And even if people were aware of it, it didn't anger them. I don't know what the difference was between Dr. Susan Moore and George Floyd—in both instances we were watching somebody on video die in front of us.

At the same time people were telling us that there were reasons to be optimistic, that a vaccine was coming, that mortality rates were down, that there's better therapeutics available—the very experimental treatments being extolled by the president were made unavailable to a Black woman who asked for them.

Our problem is twofold. We distrust medical society— and the health care establishment distrusts us. In other words, they don't believe that we're having the pains or symptoms that we're having, so how can we believe in the medical advice we're getting? How do we have a fruitful relationship? Where do we go when you don't trust us and we don't trust you? Where do we go when we've been used for experiments? Where do we go when we've been denied decent medical care?

That's the experience of all Black people. That's our relationship with doctors now. Why should we trust the medical establishment? I don't. I find myself always getting tested and retested and tested again. And I have great medical care. I have a concierge doctor, who I love and trust—but I still feel that way. And damn, it costs me money, but I'll pay it. If I look at the outcomes, I'll pay for a second opinion to make sure I didn't cheap my way into getting dead.

You gotta be able to trust your doctor and feel like you can advocate for yourself. When I had just moved to my neighborhood, West Hills, I was having these horrible stomach problems. So I found a doctor, a white guy. I went to him a couple of times, but I was still having problems. And it was weird, because he would never physically touch me. I went to him three or four times and it was almost like he was repulsed by me, literally; I'd never had a doctor who wouldn't touch me. I would think a doctor would love to touch me! I'm a fly dude. I think I'm nice. How are you gonna diagnose my problem if you don't touch me? But he never would. He would stand by the door and do an examination from there. So I had telemedicine before there actually even was telemedicine. I was a pioneer in long-distance medical care; for me, it was across the room instead of over Zoom.

So I wasn't feeling any better and I was sitting there in Dr. Brown's office. This young kid walks by and he has a lab coat on. Not literally a kid, like Doogie Howser, but a young guy. So I asked him, "Hey, man, are you a doctor?" He said yeah, so I told him about my problem and how Dr. Brown never touched me or anything. So this doctor, Dr. Lavin, did my blood workup, found out I had gastritis or something minor, and got it squared away. But because he listened to me, he became my doctor. Then he got a concierge service and now he's the doctor to several stars.

But the instant a doctor touched me and started talking to me, I started getting better. You have to be an advocate for your own health. But also, you need a doctor to listen to you and take you seriously. And my old doctor had never had any Black patients. He would order tests that are calibrated for old white men, not fly young Black dudes. So you could have a test with a level that could be low for you or high for you, but because it's beyond the baseline of what white men test at, it might not register as a problem. And then, he was missing a level of compassion and relatability. He couldn't relate to me.

But it all started because Dr. Brown wouldn't touch me. Well, years later Dr. Brown and I ended up as members of the same country club. He found out who I was and that I had been a patient of his. And then he saw me on the golf course and asked me why I stopped seeing him. So I told him about how he seemed like he didn't want to touch me, and that I wasn't getting any better. And he just said, "Oh." We never did play a round together.

BLACK BODIES ARE HAZARDOUS TO OUR HEALTH

Bias can deny you care. Racist ideas about differences in Black bodies actually get people killed. And it isn't just in medicine.

Look at how many Black kids drown in America. According to the USA Swimming Foundation, 64 percent of Black children don't know how to swim. There are around four thousand drowning deaths in the U.S. each year, but Black kids drown at a rate five and a half times higher than white kids. This is because of the racist history of pool access and lack of swimming education in America. Anyone can learn to swim, but only if you're allowed in the water. And if parents weren't allowed to swim or never learned, they're less likely to teach their kids.

In the 1920s and 1930s there was a boom in public pool building. But these pools were not for everyone. Thousands of pools were opened, but they were disproportionally for white people only. In St. Louis, as an example, Black people had access to only one small indoor pool, while white people were able to swim at nine city pools.

Even in cities where pools were not officially segregated, white people often prevented Black people from swimming in their pools through violence. Where they were forced to integrate, white people often made private club pools where they could discriminate. Black people weren't allowed to go to beaches. They weren't allowed to go to swimming pools. Nobody was teaching Black kids to swim.

One of the signature images of the civil rights era is of a motel manager dumping muriatic acid into a pool of Black activists staging a "swim-in" at the Monson Motor Lodge pool in St. Augustine, Florida. This sort of violence was in line with the racist view of Black bodies as "dirty." Racists went to great lengths to prevent "dirty" Black bodies from being in the same water as white people, for fear of contamination. The author of *Contested Waters: A Social History of Swimming Pools in America,* Jeff Wiltse, argues that white men feared that Black men would try to assault white women in the intimate environment of swimming pools. This racist fear of Black brutes lusting after white women has reared its ugly head throughout American history.

So first you make it so we can't go swimming. Then, because Black people aren't swimming, you say "they can't swim" and you chalk it up to biology. Then you broadcast these kinds of stereotypes and reinforce them. On *Nightline* with host Ted Koppel in 1987, Al Campanis, then general manager of the Los Angeles Dodgers, was defending the lack of diversity in baseball management when he said, "Why are Black men, or Black people, not good swimmers? Because they don't have the buoyancy." There's a long history of white sports authorities airing their pet theories of the biological difference between the races. For example, in 1988, Jimmy "the Greek" Snyder said that the difference between Blacks and whites "goes all the way back to the Civil War when, during the slave period, the slave owner would breed his big Black with his big woman so that he could have a big Black kid—that's where it all started. The Black is a better athlete to begin with because he's been bred to be that way because of his thigh size and big size."

That's some pernicious shit. It's not our skill or hard work, it's our biology. And if we drown, well, we're not buoyant enough. The perception becomes a limitation. What changes that perception is having role models like Simone Manuel, one of two Black women on the U.S. Olympic swimming team, who won a gold medal in Rio in the 2018 Olympics. So of course we can learn how to swim. Hell, Black people are some of the most buoyant people I know! But swimming is still a very white sport, still a predominantly white leisure activity, because of history.

It's like tennis. You can't drown on a tennis court, unless you're really trying. But before the Williams sisters, tennis seemed like it was a white sport. The barriers to entry were high for Venus and Serena. They learned to play on courts not too far from where I grew up, with glass all over the ground. Their dad had to sweep it all up for them. But would anyone say Black people can't play tennis now?

When the culture tells you that you're dirty all the time, or that you smell bad or aren't fully human, you suffer consequences. Because Hispanic and Black women were being told that they had body odor, they bought into beauty products like Johnson & Johnson baby powder at a higher rate than white women. Nobody wants to smell offensive, and the marketing campaigns were geared toward "feeling fresh."

Baby powder isn't actually used on babies that much anymore. In the 1970s, doctors starting warning people that babies could inhale talc. By the mid-2000s, 91 percent of baby powder use was by adults. Black women use the hell out of this stuff. Even my wife used to put this shit all over her; we'd have baby powder every-goddamn-where.

The problem is that baby powder turns out to be a carcinogen, which researchers have known since at least the seventies. In 2006, the World Health Organization started classifying talc as a "possible carcinogen" when women used it as a genital antiperspirant and deodorant. But instead of pulling their product, Johnson & Johnson used their marketing dollars to gain more Black women customers. They distributed samples through churches and beauty salons and ran ad campaigns targeted at "curvy Southern women 18–49 skewing African American," according to an investigation by Reuters.

Every company's gonna market its products to long-time customers, but it was a racist mentality that fed into where Johnson & Johnson decided to focus. A 1992 internal memo showed that they sought to "investigate ethnic (African American, Hispanic) opportunities to grow the franchise." The same memo also cited as a "major obstacle" that the "negative publicity from the health community on talc (inhalation, dust, negative doctor endorsement, cancer linkage) continues." Yeah, that's some negative publicity all right. Doctors say it's not safe for babies and might cause cancer, but it's still okay to market to people of color. Can you imagine them trying to get more white female customers, knowing what they did?

In the last several years, multiple women have sued Johnson & Johnson. In June 2020, a Missouri appeals court ordered the company to pay $2.1 billion in damages to women who sued after developing ovarian cancer. And multiple lawsuits continue over asbestos found in baby powder products. Maybe it's just coincidence, but in May 2020, Johnson & Johnson announced that they'd be discontinuing sales of Johnson's Baby Powder in the U.S. and Canada.

BLACK BODIES ARE GOOD FOR US

Even when you increase access to care, you're still facing implicit bias and mistrust. One of the best things we could do to fix health care for Black people would be to get more Black doctors and nurses.

Patients are more likely to listen to their doctor's recommendations if they're comfortable with the doctor. This is what the president of Morehouse College, Valerie Montgomery Rice, calls "cultural competence." Black male doctors caring for Black men leads to greater compliance with recommendations and treatment, which yields better health outcomes. So Black people are more likely to listen to Black doctors. And Black doctors are less likely to be biased against Black patients. One study randomly assigned 1,300 Black patients to a set of doctors. Those who saw Black doctors received 34 percent more preventive care than those that didn't.

But there aren't enough Black doctors. Black people make up 13 percent of the population, but only 5 percent of doctors. Dr. Montgomery Rice laid out some stark statistics in an interview with the *Wall Street Journal*. In 2018, out of twenty-one thousand students entering med school, only fifteen hundred were Black. And less than half of those were men. Overall, the ratio of Black women to Black men in med school is three to one. In all other demographics, the gender ratio is fifty-fifty. So there aren't enough Black doctors being trained and there are even fewer Black male doctors.

There's a problem with the pipeline to med schools that we have to fix. When Black boys are disproportionately punished in school and not encouraged in the sciences and math, they don't continue on to take the MCAT and become doctors. Morehouse is one of the colleges putting money and focus into recruiting and retaining more Black men for med school.

Mental health is another area where mistrust of the medical establishment has intersected with a lack of representation. Black people have not historically been included in neuroscience research. Most genetic research uses data from white people. Black and brown people make up only about 5 percent of the people involved in genetics research studies.

But Black people are about 20 percent more likely to have serious mental health problems and twice as likely to develop Alzheimer's disease. That has led to initiatives like the African Ancestry Neuroscience Research Initiative, a partnership between the Lieber Institute for Brain Development and the Black community of Baltimore. The Lieber Institute is making sure Black people are part of brain research studies—they compared the molecular makeup of about three hundred African American brains to about one thousand brains from people of European ancestry. Sounds like that Parliament song "Dr. Funkenstein."

By studying the genetic makeup of these brains, researchers hope to figure out why Alzheimer's develops more often in Black people. And some genes are less prevalent in brains from people of African descent, so there may be treatments that can be developed from understanding these differences.

BLAX VAX

And as they roll out coronavirus vaccines, we have to reckon with the fact that mistrust of a vaccine is real in the Black community. It can't be that we get blamed for dying of COVID because we gotta go to work and then get blamed for dying of COVID because we wouldn't take the vaccine.

On my radio show, we asked listeners whether they would trust a vaccine, and in twenty-four hours the segment had seventeen thousand comments. People don't trust the government to not be duplicitous. They don't want their children to get the vaccine. A poll by the Pew Research Center in September 2020 found that of those polled, only 32 percent of Black people said they would take the vaccine, compared with 52 percent of white people. As one person in a *New York Times* article about vaccine trial outreach in the Black communities of Pittsburgh put it, "I won't be used as a guinea pig for white people."

Recently, the presidents of two historically Black colleges in New Orleans, Dillard University and Xavier University of Louisiana, solicited help from their students and faculty to be part of the vaccine trials for COVID-19. And they noted the harm done to people of color by previous medical research in their appeal, because Black people have had a problem with trusting medical trials ever since Tuskegee. They said, "It is of the utmost importance that a significant number of Black and brown subjects participate so that the effectiveness of these vaccines be understood across the many diverse populations that comprise these United States."

And I can see the pros and cons of it, but we can't keep letting the white medical establishment hand us things without knowing how they affect us. We just don't believe that they have our best interests at heart, and they never believe what we're saying anyway. So I think it's great that HBCUs are getting involved. They gotta recruit from Howard, not Harvard. We gotta test members of the Divine Nine, not just the Hasty Pudding Club. Because all humans are the same, but not everybody's a white man.

When my sister had colon cancer, she was told that there was a treatment for it. And you know why? Because she was lucky enough to get the cancer that old white men get. Millions of research dollars had gone into studying it and developing treatment. She got the lucky cancer. The old white cancer.

Let me tell you something: There'll never be a cure for

sickle cell anemia unless they work to cure something else and they go, "Hey! By the way, it cures sickle cell." No one will ever deliberately research cures for anything that primarily affects us. Ever. *Did you know that this formulation that we had to cure Parkinson's in dogs actually works on niggers too and can cure sickle cell? We dared that dude in the lab to drink that shit and it cured his fucking sickle cell.*

It's a shame that Viagra didn't cure sickle cell, because you know how many great things have been discovered so white men could have hard dicks? *"Hey, don't throw that out yet! Yes, that's a terrible vasodilator. Don't throw that out. My heart still hurts, but my dick is hard as fuck."*

So in a country that thinks we're less than human, that tried to breed us out, that continues to give us worse care than white people, it's somehow our fault that we're dying of COVID? Even when we're dying, America always finds a way to make it our fault.

Trump's Health and Human Services secretary Alex Azar was maybe even clearer than Jerome Adams in blaming us for our own COVID deaths: "Unfortunately, the

American population is a very diverse— It is a population with significant unhealthy comorbidities that do make many individuals in our communities, in particular African American, minority communities, particularly at risk here because of significant underlying disease health disparities and disease comorbidities."

Trump and his supporters always tried to downplay the deaths caused by his incompetence, by saying that people aren't really dying of COVID—they're dying of other problems, but also happened to have COVID. This is another way of saying, "Hey niggers, stop smoking and drinking. Stop eating so much and getting diabetes." It's blaming us for our own deaths, as if personal responsibility is how we ended up with the unfair medical system we have. "Comorbidities" are just how Black people exist in America. So when we get blamed for dying of COVID because of "comorbidities," understand that these poor health conditions aren't because of a lack of personal responsibility; the medical system isn't set up for us. And our health is tied directly into the places we've been allowed to live, the care we've been allowed to have, and the systems that have perpetuated inequity.

PART III

PREDISPOSED TO BAD LIVING AND LEARNING

WE GET THE DIRT

Everybody's worried about the coronavirus, and rightfully so, but more Black and brown kids will die over the next few years from Trump's environmental policy rollbacks. Because whatever's the dirtiest, we get.

Growing up in my neighborhood of South Central L.A., I knew eight people who had cancer in a three-block radius. And nobody ever came and found out why. Eight people! That's a cluster, isn't it? My sister. My across-the-street neighbors: the mother and son had cancer. Next door to them: they had cancer. Next door to me: they had cancer. My father had cancer and died of it. My whole neighborhood is fucking riddled with cancer, and nobody has done anything about it. I guarantee you: in my neighborhood there are probably dozens of cases of cancer. If there was a cluster like that anywhere else, what would happen? Come on now.

It's been obvious for a long time now that the government has almost no interest in protecting people of color from environmental racism. The U.S. Environmental Protection Agency even has an Office of Civil Rights whose express purpose is to enforce the Civil Rights Act. Despite that, the U.S. Commission on Civil Rights found that by 2016, "EPA's Office of Civil Rights has never made a formal finding of discrimination and has never denied or withdrawn financial assistance from a recipient in its entire history, and has no mandate to demand accountability within the EPA." In almost three hundred cases, the EPA did nothing.

What kind of complaints get sent to the EPA's Office of Civil Rights? In one example, residents of Uniontown, Alabama, filed a complaint about a landfill that had been permitted to take coal ash from Tennessee. Coal ash is toxic, but was reclassified as "nonhazardous" by the Alabama Department of Environmental Management so that it could be disposed of in Uniontown. After the landfill started taking coal ash, residents started having headaches, breathing problems, and mental health issues. Does it surprise you to learn that Uniontown has a population that is mostly poor and Black? And does it shock you to learn that the EPA found no "causal connection" between the coal ash and the town's health problems?

A report by the Environmental Integrity Project found that "groundwater near 242 of the 265 [coal] power plants with monitoring data contained unsafe levels of one or more of the pollutants in coal ash, including arsenic, a known carcinogen, and lithium, which is associated with neurological damage, among other pollutants." And the Trump administration's EPA, led by a former coal lobbyist, tried to roll back regulations on coal ash. We didn't do anything wrong, but we get coal in our stockings. And in our food. And in our water.

But you don't have to be exposed to coal ash or live next to a freeway to get cancer. And if you do get cancer, I hope you're white, because if you're Black, it's not looking good for you.

Because even though Black and white people get cancer at a similar rate, Black people die from cancer at the highest rate of any racial or ethnic group in America. According to the American Cancer Society, the main driver of this high rate is the lower socioeconomic status of Black Americans.

If you're poor and don't have good health insurance, or any health insurance at all, you're more likely to be diagnosed with cancer too late and die from it. In 2017, Black people were twice as likely to have no health insurance as white people. Add to that a dirty environment, and you've got a lot of people dying.

WHERE WE GET TO LIVE

I don't know if people who didn't grow up in an area like I did can understand. I was nineteen years old before I realized white people lived in Los Angeles. I'm not even kidding. A friend of mine who had a car picked me up and we went for a drive. We passed this sign that said "Now Entering West Los Angeles" and it was like a totally different country. I went, "This is where white people live?"

See, when I was growing up, how you got in trouble was you went to neighborhoods you didn't belong in. But nothing was in our neighborhoods. Nothing. No grocery stores, no movie theaters, no parks, nothing. So in order to do any of those things, you had to venture out of your neighborhood. And the minute you did, you had some police officers jamming you up, saying, "What are you doing here?" Well, motherfucker, how am I going to get groceries? I gotta get some eggs and flour, man. I need Pop-Tarts. How am I gonna see the latest *Fast and the Furious*? How am I going to do anything? You know what I mean?

People in Westwood would never recognize where I lived. Where I lived was a dirty, underfunded neighborhood. We didn't have adequate resources for school. We didn't have acceptable access to necessities. It was a physically toxic environment where people got sick from cancer and asthma and a whole host of afflictions. Everything was dirty. All of my neighborhood was surrounded by factories that spewed stuff in the air and dumped stuff in the water. And obviously we know that these kinds of pollutants negatively impact our development socially, mentally, and academically.

Growing up, I had childhood asthma. All of my brothers and sisters—we all had childhood asthma. They told me I'd grow out of it, but I didn't grow out of it. I *moved* out of it: to a new neighborhood without the same environmental problems.

We didn't choose this. Our families literally couldn't

live anywhere else. We could only live in these places. The pollution, the cancer rates, and the poverty are the legacy of systemic racism. Even though segregation is illegal now, its effects are still with us in a whole host of ways.

Researchers from the National Community Reinvestment Coalition, the University of Richmond, and the University of Wisconsin–Milwaukee recently published a study analyzing historic redlining maps from cities across America created by the Home Owner's Loan Corporation in the 1930s and connecting them to current social vulnerability. These maps were created by the federal government to assess the creditworthiness of neighborhoods and set the terms of mortgages. The areas with the highest numbers of Black people and immigrants were colored red on the maps and thus were "red-lined." In redlined neighborhoods, it was almost impossible to buy or refinance a home. This lack of lending led to deteriorating housing conditions and increased health hazards.

Researchers took these old maps and compared them to the current poverty levels and health outcomes in these neighborhoods. All this time later, these formerly redlined neighborhoods still have higher poverty, shorter average life spans, and higher rates of chronic diseases. Life expectancy was almost four years lower in these communities than in communities that were highly rated by the HOLC. But it could be even starker than that; in one example cited by NPR, the average life expectancy of the predominantly Black East End neighborhood of Richmond, Virginia, was just sixty-eight years. The rich, white West End neighborhood a few miles away had a life expectancy of eighty-nine years. Just by crossing town, you could live an extra twenty-one years.

The maps from the HOLC cite "infiltration of Negroes" as one of the reasons for redlining an area. Areas that were already somewhat segregated only became more so, as white people moved out of areas without access to credit and were able to build wealth through homeownership in ways Black people in a redlined community could not. And even though redlining was abolished in 1968 by the Fair Housing Act, its effects are still with us.

In fact, fewer Black people owned homes in 2019 than owned homes when segregation was legal. So instead of working to remedy this, the Trump administration doubled down on this segregation by repealing the Affirmatively

Furthering Fair Housing rule that Barack Obama put in place. The AFFH rule required Housing and Urban Development to come up with plans to counteract housing discrimination in areas that received federal housing funds. Ben Carson, Trump's lackey at HUD, suspended the rule in 2018, and then Trump got rid of it in July 2020 as part of his pitch to racist white voters. Remember how he kept saying Biden wanted to "abolish the suburbs"? That was Trump's way of dog-whistling to white suburban women that they wouldn't have to worry about pesky Black people moving into their white enclaves. "I am happy to inform all of the people living their Suburban Lifestyle Dream that you will no longer be bothered or financially hurt by having low income housing built in your neighborhood... Your housing prices will go up based on the market, and crime will go down. I have rescinded the Obama-Biden AFFH Rule. Enjoy!" he tweeted.

It doesn't get clearer than that, does it? If you let the Black people in, crime will follow. Your "Suburban Lifestyle Dream" will become a nightmare. But for Black and brown people suffering the ramifications of racist housing policy, the nightmare continues. Redlining leads to divestment and segregation. Housing stock deteriorates; access to good food, schools, banks, and transportation decreases. Health outcomes worsen. And then when we try to move, try to improve our situation, we're blamed for increasing crime and lowering housing values.

But Trump has a long history with housing discrimination because housing discrimination was the family business. In 2017, the FBI released records from its investigation of the Trump family business from the 1970s. The Civil Rights Division filed a suit against the Trump Management Company in 1973 alleging discrimination against Blacks and Puerto Ricans trying to rent apartments. The complaint contains details like a doorman who told agents that "if a Black person came to 2650 Ocean Parkway and inquired about an apartment for rent, and he, that is [redacted] was not there at the time, that I should tell him that the rent was twice as much as it really was, in order that he could not afford the apartment." The FBI and Trump ended up entering into a consent decree in 1975 that required the company to put safeguards into place. But even after that, the Justice Department accused them of violating the consent decree and steering Black tenants into only a handful of properties.

WHERE WE GET TO LEARN

Recently I went back to my old elementary school, Avalon Gardens, to hand out masks to the children. And the school looked exactly the same as it did when I grew up there. Everything's the same: It's literally the same color, same terrible classrooms, the same everything. The library is the same one-room library that I grew up with. It's still got maybe three hundred books, tops. I bet if you opened up *Where the Wild Things Are,* you'd see my name on the library check-out card.

Brown v. Board of Education was decided in 1954, but America's schools are still largely segregated. Sixty-seven years ago, the Supreme Court said, "Separate educational facilities are inherently unequal," but that's still what we have today. A 2019 report by the educational nonprofit EdBuild showed that the majority of kids go to schools that are in racially concentrated districts, where over 75 percent of students are either white or nonwhite. And nationwide the districts that serve Black and brown kids receive $23 billion less than mostly white districts. That's an average of $2,200 less per kid.

And when I looked out at the schoolyard, it hit me how

much it looked like a prison yard. It was just a concrete slab; nothing that would make it feel fun for kids. You see some of these suburban white schools and the playgrounds are something out of Dr. Seuss; they have colorful slides and climbing equipment, sprinklers and crazy, spinning plastic shit you can climb all over. You come out of playing on something like that full of wonder, feeling like *I'm gonna go work at Google!*

My old schoolyard looks just like a jail. There's a dude in the corner lifting weights and another guy stacking tires for some reason. It's tough being a kid these days. Then I imagine all the people who have been through there; it's like they're being prepared to go to a supermax.

I didn't go to elementary school yesterday. Why hasn't anything improved? It's actually gotten worse than when I went there. When I went there, there was a school next door to Avalon Gardens called Benjamin Banneker Special Education Center for kids with learning disabilities. The kids would sometimes have to eat at our school or we'd have to go eat at theirs. But now, the resources have been cut so much that they've closed that one down and combined the two schools. It's even more crowded.

And even though it's still a mostly Black neighborhood

and most of the kids are Black, now is the first time that they've had a Black male principal.

It's interesting to go back there. How many children in that neighborhood and the neighborhood where I grew up had cancer or asthma? Imagine if you grew up in that environment; it's already economically starved and the schools are underfunded in every way.

So to act as if that doesn't have an impact on learning or on health? These are the situations that we are born into. If you look at large cities, the people in prison have lead in their blood. Were they predisposed to criminality? Or were there environmental impacts that helped them along the way?

We know so much more about the impacts of lead poisoning than we used to. The Environmental Protection Agency mandated the phasing out of leaded gasoline in 1973 and lead paint was banned in 1978. Researchers have shown that air-lead levels peaked in the early seventies as well, falling afterward.

Lead has been shown to cause a variety of cognitive and behavioral problems. Lab animals exposed to lead are more prone to aggression. It messes up brain development and interferes with the dopamine system that regulates reward and impulse behavior.

Many scientists believe that the drop in violent crime in the 1990s wasn't due to "broken windows policing," but because of the absence of lead. The CDC says that 5 micrograms of lead per deciliter of blood is an abnormal level. But in 1976, Americans' average level was 16 micrograms per deciliter. By 1991, that had dropped to 3 micrograms. In the sixties, the CDC's "acceptable" lead level was set at 60 micrograms, then cut down to 40 in 1970, then 10 in 1991. Imagine the change that has made. So kids born in the mid-to-late seventies had a lot less lead in their bodies than kids born before that.

The Cincinnati Lead Study tracked 300 children born in areas of Cincinnati that typically had higher levels of lead exposure, starting in the late 1970s. By measuring blood-lead levels over time, the study showed that by 2008, 250 members of the lead study had been arrested 800 times. The average blood-lead level of a participant during their childhood correlated with their arrest rate.

Ruth Ann Norton, the executive director of the Coalition to End Childhood Lead Poisoning, told the *Washington*

Post, "A child who was poisoned with lead is seven times more likely to drop out of school and six times more likely to end up in the juvenile justice system." The dirty environment is literally creating criminals.

BATTLE OF THE BANDS

So we get more lead and less money. In California, voters passed Proposition 13 in 1978, a ballot measure that slashed the amount of money available to local schools. At my school in the late seventies, we used to have after-school programs and school lunch programs and summer programs. But after Prop 13 passed, everything was gutted.

We used to get bused to school, but then they took the buses away. They took the after-school programs away. They took the free lunch programs away. They took the summer job programs away.

I grew up on 135th and Avalon. The buses took us from my neighborhood in the unincorporated part of Los Angeles to schools in Gardena. Peary Junior High was my junior high school and Gardena High was my high school.

But after they cut the buses, we had to walk to school.

All the kids from my neighborhood had to walk through these gang-controlled areas every day, there and back. All of us would walk together, like twenty or thirty of us. From my house to Gardena High was a good six or seven miles. Imagine walking through all of the gang neighborhoods. You ever see those nature specials where the crocodiles are waiting for the water buffaloes to cross the river? All of the buffaloes are at the edge of the water, going like, "No, dude, you go first!" And the crocodiles are just hanging out with their eyes peeping above water, waiting for a snack. It was like that. Sometimes you got lucky and you'd get a bus pass and you could ride the city bus. But if your mother and father didn't have no fucking money, you had to walk.

And over time, the herd got thinned out, you know? Eventually, all the dudes who could fight from our neighborhood got kicked out of school for defending themselves. So, in the end, all you got are these dudes who can't fight. Now it's just a bunch of band nerds. You try to get through the Shotgun Crips with a dude who plays the fucking oboe. I mean, you don't have much of a chance when the dudes you're running with only have tubas and oboes and violins. *Reggie, quick, hit 'em with an F-sharp!*

Now, a lot of them motherfuckers went on to become successful musicians too. But these dudes weren't doing anything wrong. They just lived in our neighborhoods; they weren't with the shit we were with. They weren't hanging out, smoking weed. But they still would get their asses whooped too. These dudes weren't predisposed to violence; these dudes were predisposed to bad transportation.

And if you got into fights, a lot of times you dropped out of school. That's what happened to me. I got kicked out of school. I got into a beef with some dudes on the way to school that spilled over into school, so I got kicked out of Gardena High in tenth grade. Then I went to Locke High. Then I got kicked out of Locke High. Then I went to San Pedro High. I got kicked out of San Pedro High because, again, I had to ride this bus through all these neighborhoods with all these dudes who fucking hated me. Then I went to Gardena Adult School. I'm sixteen years old and I've been kicked out of Gardena, Locke, and San Pedro.

So now I can only go to school at night, so I show up to Gardena Adult night school. And I was determined. I said to myself, *I'm going to get my life together. I'm tired of getting my ass whooped. I'm tired of switching high schools. I gotta get a job.* This dude Curtis came to me and some other dudes because one of the security guards was flirting with his girlfriend. So they get into a fight and we start fighting these dudes who are the security guards at the adult school. What we didn't know was that the security guards were Gardena policemen. We had no idea. We fought the fucking police. The next day several police cars from Gardena Police Department came up to the school. The cops said, "You niggers meet us in the graveyard and we'll fight it out." This officially ended my educational journey, because I never went to school again.

But I guarantee you, I'm not unique. Was I predisposed to violence? No, there are lots of people like me. They were in school. They liked it. They were going to school, doing after-school programs and such. And then, all of those resources are taken away from them, and what do they do? What do they do? And then you see this huge spike in crime in Los Angeles. So, were we violent, unteachable children from the start, or did we become that?

My story is notable only in that I ascended past that. What isn't unique is that if you go through my experiences growing up, everybody you know is either dead or in jail. Now, is that because we were inherently criminal? Were we predisposed to be that way, or was it the environmental impacts that were forced upon us? What was it? And these same circumstances are replicated in every urban environment across the country.

We know that when Black children go to parochial schools they do better than other races. And if they are enrolled in early education programs like Head Start, they perform at a higher level than any other demographic or ethnicity.

So the notion that we're somehow biologically unable to learn can't be correct. If that were true, how could you take somebody from Nigeria, or somebody from the West Indies, and bring them here and have them excel? These are people of color raised in a different culture who come here and they succeed. When brown or Black people come to this country, they're here to take advantage of our educational system. So they might be a cabdriver now, but they're also a molecular scientist.

Or if people are biologically predisposed, what about other countries? Look at India: sixty to seventy years ago it was a very poor country, but now it's become an educational power. Why is that?

And meanwhile, the white people here are getting dumber. How else do you explain Trump boat parades,

QAnon, and *The Real Housewives of Orange County*? Do you all really want to compare notes?

GETTING KICKED OUT OF NO SCHOOL

Black students in America still get a raw deal. We get expelled from school at a higher rate than whites and are disciplined more often. Black boys are almost four times more likely to be given out-of-school suspensions than white boys. Black girls are five times more likely to be suspended than white girls.

Even in the COVID era, where kids are *already* not in school, administrators are finding ways to kick them out of school. I mean, how do you kick someone out of school who's already out? With a Zoom suspension, of course. A Black fourth grader in Sacramento had her email privileges suspended after she asked for help. And if you're a kid in Shelby County, Tennessee, make sure you're looking sharp on your Zoom call because there's still a school dress code for virtual learning. It's okay to set your Zoom to look like you're flying around in space, but make sure you've got "appropriate dress" on, or you can still be suspended from not-school.

But getting suspended isn't as bad as getting thrown in prison, right? A Black fifteen-year-old in Michigan was sentenced by a judge to a juvenile detention facility after she didn't do her homework. This girl was originally on probation for a physical altercation she had with her mother. But even though the whole country was shut down due to COVID, the judge held an in-person hearing. The girl's lawyer participated by Zoom. And even though the Michigan guidelines during COVID called for minimizing detentions amid prison outbreaks, the judge found the girl guilty "on failure to submit any schoolwork and getting up for school." The judge ordered her to a detention center because she was "a threat to community," saying that not doing her online homework was a violation of the terms of her parole. Homework is for learning sentence structure, not the structure of sentencing guidelines. You're not supposed to learn math by calculating your prison term, right?

Kicking kids out of school has huge negative impacts. Kids obviously don't learn as well when they can't go to school. And if they're not learning, they don't do as well academically and that leads to worse job opportunities and so on.

So is it just that Black kids act out more? This is where America always likes to place the blame: Why can't Black kids stop acting up, stop listening to rap, pull their saggy pants up, and pull themselves up by their bootstraps? Maybe they need more *discipline;* maybe the only way to correct for the deficiencies in the Black culture is to instill discipline like some of the charter school systems try to impart. Stand still, don't talk, get in line—like you're being prepped for the army, not to learn. Or maybe you're being prepped for prison.

Or is it racial bias from the teachers? Studies have shown that implicit bias in teachers starts as early as preschool. A Yale study showed a conference of preschool teachers a set of videos with four children: a Black boy and girl and a white boy and girl. They asked the teachers to be on the lookout for bad behavior, but the videos didn't show any bad behavior. Still, eye scans showed that teachers watched the Black boy the most, expecting something bad to happen. When you're looking for bad behavior, you find it. And that's why Black preschoolers get suspended more often than white preschoolers.

PART IV

PREDISPOSED TO VIOLENCE

As I wrote in *How Not to Get Shot*, the most dangerous place for a Black person to live is in a white person's imagination. The racism and bias are deeply ingrained in America. Implicit bias, racist policies, and the effects of historical inequities have kept Black people in America living more dangerous lives than white people. The threats *to* us are many—bad health care, bad housing, bad schooling—but in contemporary America we're treated like the threat. Because white people are predisposed to believe Black people are violent.

KAREN NATION

When Donald Trump made his appeal to suburban women, he was channeling some big Karen energy. All that "end of the suburbs" stuff is just about continuing to tell us where we can do what we do.

The most egregious thing that arises with the Karens is that we're prejudged as not belonging wherever we're at. Nowadays, more Black people live in the suburbs than live in the cities. Basically, Black people and white people are living around each other more than we used to, but somehow Black people are always looked upon like we don't belong.

And City Karens are as accustomed to using their power as Suburban Karens. Probably the most famous example was when Amy Cooper called the cops on Christian Cooper in Central Park in 2020. Christian Cooper was bird-watching and asked her to put her dog on a leash. Then she called the cops, saying, "I'm going to tell them there's an African American man threatening my life."

Now, I gotta admit that if I were a police officer, and I was called to the scene and a white woman told me that a nigga was bird-watching, I'd be on guard. Everything I know about niggas and bird-watching, they came by the kilo. *That's the gram bird, that's the ounce bird, that's the kilo bird.* Yeah, usually the Black dudes I know ain't watching birds. They're flipping them.

But I guess I've got a lot to learn about bird-watching.

Maybe I'll buy some binoculars. And meanwhile, a Black dude could have been killed by the police just because a white woman didn't want to leash her dog. Because we're predisposed to be violent.

The Karens are there to tell us where we can and can't be. That what we're up to is suspect. And to let us know the consequences if we don't listen to them. They yell at us in stores, in parking lots, at the park, in our buildings, at our schools, and at the pool. They come at us, maskless, spitting hate and calling us *nigger*. The consequences aren't always as dire as they were for Emmett Till, but that's the history for us—white women accusing us of something we didn't do and us paying with our lives.

VIOLENT KARENS

I don't know if you can call the rednecks who killed Ahmaud Arbery "Karens," because I've never seen a Karen with a beard and a beer gut, but when William Bryan, Gregory McMichael, and Travis McMichael chased Ahmaud down in their pickup truck, they were acting like a bunch of Violent Karens. Ahmaud didn't "look like he belonged" in their neighborhood, and so this posse decided to trap him and confront him as he was out jogging. Of course, these guys decided that he "fit the description" of a burglary suspect.

And yet, when two vehicles surrounded him in Satilla Shores, Georgia, and several fat white guys with guns jumped out and said, "Stop, stop, we want to talk to you," Ahmaud didn't feel like talking. Crazy, right?

After Ahmaud was killed, the police report gave us some details about what went down: "McMichael stated they pulled up beside the male and shouted stop again at which time Travis exited the truck with the shotgun. Mc-Michael stated the unidentified male began to violently attack Travis and the two men then started fighting over the shotgun at which point Travis fired a shot and then a second later there was a second shot. McMichael stated the male fell face down on the pavement with his hand under his body. McMichael stated he rolled the man over to see if the male had a weapon." Turns out that Ahmaud hadn't been out jogging with a gun tucked in his running shorts. A guy in a pickup truck jumps out with a shotgun, but the unarmed jogger is the one who "violently attacked" someone? It makes no sense.

Except that it made perfect sense to the cops. These good ole boys just lynched Ahmaud like they used to do. You see, Gregory McMichael is an ex-cop with ties to the DA's office. So he's allowed to dole out vigilante justice as he sees fit. The cops let Ahmaud Arbery's killers walk free and didn't charge them with anything. And why would they? Don't you see? Ahmaud was in *the wrong neighborhood* and he *fit the description* and he *attacked them*.

Or as district attorney George Barnhill put it, "Given the fact Arbery initiated the fight, at the point Arbery grabbed the shotgun, under Georgia Law, McMichael was allowed to use deadly force to protect himself." That's why the McMichaels were allowed to go home that day, even though they had just killed a dude in broad daylight.

And then there was the cover-up. It's always the same: "Nothing to see here." The police called Ahmaud's mother and told her that her son had been involved in a robbery and had been killed by "the homeowner." The first district attorney assigned to the case recused herself because she had worked with Gregory McMichael, so she assigned it to George Barnhill, who decided that there was "insufficient probable cause" to issue arrest warrants. Then he had to recuse himself because his son had worked with Gregory

McMichael. It was only under a new DA and after video of Arbery's killing leaked that the Georgia Bureau of Investigation and the FBI got involved, finally charging the McMichaels and Bryan.

All these cops, all these DAs knew each other and covered up for each other. This same DA had tried to prosecute a Black woman for helping a first-time voter use a voting machine (a jury found her not guilty). The police department had been under investigation a bunch of times in the years leading up to Arbery's killing. The police chief was arrested for stonewalling an investigation looking into a narcotics task force.

And then the defense lawyers for the McMichaels set forth a bunch of requests in the lead-up to the trial: They didn't want the word "victim" to be used when referring to Ahmaud. They didn't want any pictures to be shown of him with his family, only pictures of him by himself. They didn't want family to be allowed to identify him in court. In other words, they didn't want Ahmaud Arbery to seem human. This type of attitude is exactly why the killers weren't charged with anything in the first place. What they wanted is what white people in the South used to have, what they had decades ago: a system set up to allow white people to kill Black people without consequence.

Somehow these bad cops and their pals are never to blame. Why did Ahmaud Arbery grab the shotgun and cause his own death? Somehow it's always our fault when we die.

ROLL THE TAPE

It's crazy how many Black people caused their own deaths until we get to see the tape. Once we see the evidence, it becomes a lot clearer that somebody else killed them. Ahmaud Arbery violently attacked a guy, and the guy shot him in self-defense—until we saw that Ahmaud was chased down and threatened. Then we know what happened.

Sometimes it's months or years later that we get to see the tape. The police are happy to lie to us about what happened anytime a Black person dies. Take Daniel Prude, who cops said died of a drug overdose. Except the tape shows that he didn't.

When Daniel's brother Joe called the police in Rochester, New York, he was frantically trying to get help for his brother, who had been acting weird and then dashed off into the winter night only partly clothed. Joe had tried to have his brother hospitalized earlier because he thought that Daniel was having a mental health crisis. But the hospital sent him home, and later that night he ran off.

When the police found Daniel, he was nude and yelling crazy stuff. He was obviously in distress and in need of medical attention. They restrained him and put a "spit hood" on him. These spit hoods are supposed to be used to protect officers from spitting and biting. I mean, there's a reason Black people are a little sensitive about getting restrained and then getting a hood put over their heads. That shit's straight out of a lynching postcard.

It's not just a bad look—these things are dangerous. At least ten people have died with spit hoods on in police custody since 2001. In April 2020, Tucson police killed Carlos Ingram Lopez by holding him down and covering his face with a hood. And in Sacramento, a viral video showed police putting a hood over a twelve-year old Black boy while arresting him. The family is suing the police department for $100,000.

In Daniel's case, the cops had him cuffed, put a hood

over his head, and then they kneeled on him, pushing his face into the ground. And he asphyxiated. I understand you gotta protect yourself, but what is it with driving his face into the fucking ground? What's that all about?

Police told his brother that Daniel had died of a drug overdose. Another dude who killed himself, nothing to see here. But now we know that the police tried to cover up the death by changing their reports and delaying release of the body cam footage. The police chief knew that the footage would spark protests, so the department used delay tactics and stonewalling to buy time. As a result, even though Daniel was killed in February, the video was only sent to the Prude family's lawyer in August. Without the video, we'd never know that another bunch of cops choked a guy to death who needed their help instead. Video is our only self-defense.

So I think that's what set us off with George Floyd in May 2020. They couldn't stonewall that video, and Minneapolis police officer Derek Chauvin didn't even seem to care that he was being taped. The thing with George Floyd is that we all saw what went down with our own eyes immediately. We all saw the video of Officer Chauvin kneeling on his neck for almost nine minutes as he gasped for air, said, "I can't breathe," and called for his mother. So we know what happened. It's not a mystery who killed George Floyd.

But that didn't stop white people from trying to pin some part of the blame for George Floyd's death on George Floyd himself. The medical examiner's report on the tragedy was cherry-picked to partly blame Floyd for his own death. The charging document released by authorities said that "the effects of the officers' restraint of Mr. Floyd, his underlying health conditions, and the presence of the drugs contributed to his death." So, you know, his death was a combination of things—not just a knee on his neck. That's all the conservative *Washington Times* needed to hear, running the headline "Asphyxiation Not the Cause of George Floyd's Death: Autopsy." I don't need an autopsy to know what I saw was a cop murdering a Black man.

And months later, when police body cam footage of the lead-up to the killing was leaked, Fox News commentator Tucker Carlson saw what he always sees: cops just doing their job, cops who were blameless in another Black man's death. When the cops asked Floyd if "he was on something," that was enough for Carlson to declare on national TV that the footage incriminates Floyd himself. Carlson said that Floyd had "more than enough fentanyl to die of an overdose." The only overdose I saw was an overdose of police violence. He added, "One of the best known symptoms of fentanyl overdose, by the way, is shortness of breath." Aerobics class also causes shortness of breath, but George Floyd didn't die by Jazzercise. It's the old playbook again: he was no angel, he didn't listen to police orders, he resisted arrest, we had a right to kill him.

What that body cam footage actually shows is Floyd begging not to be arrested, saying that he's scared that he'll be killed. When they roll up on him as he sits in his car, you can hear how scared he is:

"Okay, Mr. Officer, please don't shoot me. Please, man."

"I'll look at you eye-to-eye, man. Please don't shoot me, man."

"Please don't shoot me, Mr. Officer. Please, don't shoot me, man. Please. Can you not shoot me, man?"

His friend who was in the car with Floyd tried to tell the cops that George was scared of police because he'd been shot before. He was having a panic attack and freaking out because he was claustrophobic and didn't want to get in the squad car.

"I'm claustrophobic, man, please man, please."

"Please, I'm not that kind of guy, Mr. Officer. Please!"

"Please, man. Don't leave me by myself, man, please, I'm just claustrophobic, that's it."

This was a guy in distress. So do the cops help him? No, they throw him on the ground and kneel on him as he says over and over:

"I can't breathe. I can't breathe. I can't breathe."

"I can't breathe."

"I can't breathe."

"Mama, mama, mama, mama."

And when Derek Chauvin chokes him out, when we all see it on video, we hear it's his own fault, that he died from chronic medical conditions and drugs.

But what about Chauvin's background? Why do cops always have the presumption of innocence and not us? When Chauvin was brought to court, charged with second-degree murder after public pressure, we find out that he's used excessive neck restraints at least four times before. Why do cops get to brutalize us over and over? Why isn't more done about their bias and racism?

Former Los Angeles police chief Daryl Gates once said that he thought choke holds might kill more Black people because their "veins and arteries do not open as fast as they do in normal people." This is the kind of mental gymnastics police do to justify the killing of Black people. Anything to blame us for our own deaths. Our bodies are different. We're not like white people. We're predisposed to bad health, drug use, and violence. We're culpable in our own deaths.

Breonna Taylor was asleep in her own apartment, so how could she be to blame for her own death? What could she have done differently except not lived there? On March 13, 2020, Louisville cops bashed in her door and her boyfriend, Kenneth Walker, thought they were intruders, so he fired at them. When the cops fired back, they killed Breonna. No, we can't even sleep in safety.

When I lived on 135th and Avalon, if somebody crashed in my door in the middle of the night without announcing who they were, I would assume something bad was happening. And if I had a weapon, I would use it. I mean, even the Jehovah's Witnesses knock.

And whatever happened to the "castle doctrine" that white people always like to throw around when they shoot Black people? Whatever happened to "stand your ground"? It's okay for George Zimmerman to shoot Trayvon or Michael Drejka to kill Markeis McGlockton, but not for Kenneth Walker to shoot an intruder? It's okay for Amber Guyger to go into the wrong apartment and kill Botham Jean or Mark and Patricia McCloskey to aim guns at peaceful protesters and cite the castle doctrine, but not for a Black dude. So what happened when Breonna's boyfriend shot at what he thought were intruders? The cops murdered his girlfriend and then charged him with attempted murder.

To believe that the cops knocked and announced themselves properly is to believe that they did those two things correctly while doing everything else incorrectly. They were supposed to have an ambulance on standby, but they sent it away. Their warrant was executed late at night for no reason, since the main suspect was already in custody. They altered police records. They did everything wrong, but somehow we're supposed to believe they knocked and announced themselves.

It's too late for Breonna, but that's why Breonna's Law seeks to ban "no-knock" warrants and requires active body cameras when police serve a warrant.

A lot of places have already restricted or banned no-knock warrants, because the police fuck up and kill people. In 2017, the *New York Times* did an investigation that found that at least eighty-one civilians had died in raids like these between 2010 and 2016. And a lot of times, the authorities raid the wrong place and kill innocent people, including a seven-year-old girl in Detroit and a sixty-eight-year-old grandfather in Framingham, Massachusetts. And of course these are mostly Black and brown people. How the fuck do you get the address wrong for Black people? Our addresses have three numbers in them. 132 Malcolm X Boulevard. White people get rich, and then their address is like a tasting menu: 1958 Pinot Grigio Circle in Lower Hidden Valley Ranch Estates, Wyoming. That's an address that's easy to fuck up, yet nobody's raiding that place.

Why the hell didn't the police have body cameras? If they had them, why weren't they on? How is it that every other cop who showed up at the scene after the shooting had body cameras, but the dudes raiding the apartment didn't?

And in the end, what happened? A grand jury indicted one officer on charges of "wanton endangerment." And that was because he shot through a patio door and window without even looking. The two other officers who killed Breonna weren't charged with anything.

One of the officers involved in her death, Sergeant Jonathan Mattingly, sent an email out to Louisville officers defending himself and the department. "We all signed up to be police officers . . . We wanted to do the right thing in the midst of an evil world to protect those who cannot protect themselves." Who protected Breonna?

Mattingly also said, "It's sad how the good guys are demonized, and criminals are canonized." Who is he talking about? Breonna wasn't a criminal. And even if he thinks the cops are the "good guys," how are they being demonized? The only cop charged in her death was charged for "wanton endangerment," not murder. If you run a stoplight, you're charged with wanton endangerment. It's nothing. It's like hunting without a license.

I'm trying to figure out what Breonna Taylor could've

done that would've protected her. They passed Breonna's Law in Louisville, but nobody was charged with breaking it. And it didn't matter how many T-shirts had her face on them, how many magazine covers she was on, or how many athletes posted about her; none of that mattered. The only accountability we got was the equivalent of the punishment for running a stop sign and killing somebody.

I think it's interesting that when authorities want to explain why we die, they always put a Black face on it. Like, Trump's administration had hardly any Black people in it, but Jerome Adams was out there to blame us for our COVID deaths.

Or with Breonna Taylor, you've seemingly got one Black dude in Kentucky government, but he's the guy in charge of explaining why Breonna Taylor had to die: the state attorney general, Daniel Cameron. He's out there to explain and excuse the actions of racist white cops.

I hope for the best for them both. I hope Daniel Cameron gets everything he wants. I hope he lives a long, fruitful life. I hope he has children. But I hope that if something happens to his Black children, that they never seek "justice" from a man like him.

It was on the anniversary of the 1955 acquittal of the

killers of Emmett Till that Daniel Cameron announced that there'd be no charges in the murder of Breonna Taylor. On the same day in history. It feels ironic, but I'm sure that every day's a day we could commemorate a famous nigga who died. We'd run out of calendar looking for a free day. *How 'bout next Tuesday?*—Nope, that was Trayvon. *What about April 4?* C'mon, man—that was MLK! Are you serious?

If you look at the history of all these kinds of cases, they always start by saying, "There's nothing to see here." If you look at Breonna Taylor's case, initially there were three different investigations and they all said there was no crime committed.

And when Kentucky attorney general Daniel Cameron says, "What I can provide today are the facts, which my office has worked long and hard to uncover," he's lying. No, you didn't. Not until we made you follow the facts. Not until we wouldn't let up. And that's not hard to figure, because you know what the first Black attorney general of Kentucky wants to be? He wants to be the first Black governor of Kentucky or the first Black senator of Kentucky. And you do that by not irritating the power establishment. You do that by pretending that the cops didn't do anything wrong. You do that by making speeches while sitting on your hands. He didn't just come here to keep his head low; he's trying to make his mark and appeal to the white law-and-order types of Kentucky. His speech about why he couldn't charge anyone with anything is probably gonna be longer than the sentence given to the police officer for "wanton endangerment."

Instead of being outraged about Breonna's death, Cameron reserved that outrage for "celebrities, influencers, and activists, who, having never lived in Kentucky, will try to tell us how to feel, suggesting they understand the facts of this case and that they know our community and the Commonwealth better than we do. But they don't." He doesn't want "outsiders" judging Kentucky. Well, every time a Black person gets killed somewhere, I hear about "Black-on-Black crime" in Chicago. I've never lived in Chicago, but I've still gotta hear about it. Tucker Carlson's never lived in Kentucky, Kenosha, or Chicago, but he still talks about them. Sean Hannity, Bill Barr, and Donald Trump sure like to express their outrage when it suits their interests. So no, us outsiders aren't going to stop trying to fight injustice in places we don't live.

What's justice for people killed by cops? After months

of pressure and protests, Louisville agreed to pay Breonna's family a $12 million settlement, but they still didn't prosecute any of the cops involved. So there's payment, but no justice. And that's because America's always paid for Black lives. They've put a premium on Black lives; they've assigned a value to them. They're used to paying for us like chattel. It's a cost of doing business. If someone stole your slave, you could be reimbursed. If your slave died, you got insurance. America's used to paying for Black bodies. They're just not used to paying to protect them.

So you have to live a pristine life. The only way your life can matter is if you're above reproach. And even then, the cops who kill you barely get punished. This ain't new. Look at what happened to Oscar Grant in Fruitvale Station back in 2009: the cop who shot him in the back only served eleven months in jail. Dude was on the ground and the cop shot him in the back, claiming he thought he had reached for his Taser instead of his gun.

Or what happened to Malice Green in Detroit in 1992. A bunch of cops beat him to death with their flashlights and then at trial they tried to blame him for his own death. Defense lawyers tried to discredit the autopsy report by saying that even though officers had struck more than a dozen blows to Malice Green's head, the cocaine in his system was what killed him. In other words, if he hadn't been on drugs, he would've been able to sustain an ass-whooping.

BLUE-ON-BLACK CRIME

It's crazy that the people who are always invoking "Black-on-Black crime" as evidence of our violent predisposition are the same people who are always excusing violent police officers as "a few bad apples." The notion behind "Black-on-Black crime" is that crime is so inherent in Black people that everybody who lives in a Black neighborhood should be regarded as criminal. It's a racist, flawed theory. Meanwhile, if you look at the pattern of violence perpetrated by some police departments over time, it's excused in each instance.

There's bad apples, and then there's bad apple orchards. We know that some of the police departments we complain about are rife with corruption. Take the Los Angeles Police

Department: this outfit was so corrupt and violent that it was put under a federal consent decree. The LAPD and the Los Angeles County Sheriff's Department are some of the most violent law enforcement organizations in the country.

It's incredible that the video of George Floyd being murdered by a cop came almost thirty years after the video of Rodney King getting beaten by cops. Right there you've had thirty years of video evidence of police violence. Derek Chauvin in Minneapolis in 2020 is acting the same as the cops in LA in 1991.

After the Rodney King beating, an independent commission investigated the LAPD and found systemic problems that needed to be fixed. The Christopher Commission, led by Warren Christopher, found that "there is a significant number of officers in the LAPD who repetitively use excessive force against the public and persistently ignore the written guidelines of the department regarding force." The commission also reported that "the Department not only failed to deal with the problem group of officers but it often rewarded them with positive evaluations and promotions." So there it is right there: the LAPD encouraged excessive violence. And an example of a "bad apple" from the report: "One officer had 13 allegations of excessive force and improper tactics, 5 other complaint allegations, 28 use of force reports, and 1 shooting." That's one poisonous apple.

The chief of police, Daryl Gates, resigned in the wake of the uprising after the Rodney King jury verdict. Still, this guy never acknowledged that his department was out of control. He said, "Clearly that night we should have gone down there and shot a few people. In retrospect, that's exactly what we should have done. We should have blown a few heads off."

The Los Angeles Police Department was put under a consent decree that provided federal oversight of the department in 2000, after the beating of Rodney King and a series of insane police crimes that culminated in the Rampart corruption scandal.

In 1997, bank robbers stole $722,000 from a Bank of America and investigators eventually figured out that it was an inside job planned by an assistant bank manager and her boyfriend, an LAPD officer. This dude refused to say where the money went, but two days after the robbery, he and a bunch of other officers had gone gambling in Vegas with thousands of dollars.

Then in 1998, the cops upped their game. Officials discovered that one of these same cops, Rafael Perez, had stolen eight pounds of cocaine from police evidence rooms. When the detectives first questioned him, he said, "Is this about the bank robbery?" I mean, you'd think that a cop would know better than to offer up his guilt—I thought that shit only happened on TV shows. But no, this dude fessed up to a crime they weren't even asking about. But then he flipped and struck a plea deal and provided inside information on a series of other crimes committed by fellow officers in the Rampart CRASH division—an antigang unit (Community Resources Against Street Hoodlums). Perez provided testimony against about seventy officers for a number of crimes and a range of misconduct. These revelations led to 140 civil lawsuits against the city of Los Angeles and cost the city $125 million in settlements.

And even though a judge let the department out of the consent decree in 2009, studies show that officers still use force against Black and brown people more often than they do against white people. In the most recent protests after the George Floyd killing, L.A. cops were out there beating people with batons like they've always done. The *Los Ange-*

les Times reported that Black drivers are stopped at a much higher rate than their share of the population, and then they are four times more likely to be searched than a white driver who was stopped. The "elite" Metro division stops an even greater proportion of Black drivers; Connie Rice, a civil rights lawyer, called it "stop-and-frisk in a car."

And it'd be one thing if L.A. only had a single abusive, criminal law enforcement agency working within its borders. But L.A. also has the Los Angeles County Sheriff's Department, which has been the subject of multiple years of investigation for abuse of prisoners. A 2011 ACLU report found that deputies assaulted inmates, sometimes beating them for asking for medical treatment. They beat an inmate, paraded him around, and put him in a cell to be sexually assaulted. The jails are basically run by a criminal gang of deputies.

In fact, a whistleblower recently alleged that some sheriff's deputies are full-on gang members and still on the force. The complaint details how a group of deputies with skull tattoos and Nazi symbols called "the Executioners" ran the Compton station. According to Art Gonzalez, the deputy who filed the complaint, this gang controls scheduling, assignments, and distribution of informant tips. These "inked" members have been involved in shootings and beatings. A history of gangs in the sheriff's department has been documented over the years, including groups named the Vikings, the Reapers, the Jump Out Boys, and the Banditos.

Defenders of these gangs call them "cliques" and say they boost morale and camaraderie. So they're like the Shriners for cops? The Shriners drive around in tiny cars, wear red fezzes, and give money to hospitals. They don't whoop your ass or shoot you five times in the back, like the two deputies who killed Andres Guardado in June 2020. Guardado was working as a security guard at an auto body shop in Gardena when he was shot by a deputy in an alley for "having a gun." There's no body camera footage of the killing and the officers somehow haven't found any video footage from surrounding businesses. Huh.

We've got police who are in gangs, but Black people are predisposed to violence? How are the police supposed to be reformed to be less violent when they are themselves criminal? So you've got gang members shaking down gang members, exacerbating tensions, bringing violence to our streets instead of preventing violence.

The previous sheriff, Lee Baca, was sentenced to prison for obstructing a federal investigation into corruption and civil rights abuses at county jails. The FBI began investigating the county, and instead of cooperating, Sheriff Baca ordered investigations of the agents investigating him. The undersheriff, Paul Tanaka, was put in charge of a scheme to hide an informant and engage in witness tampering. Both of these dudes were indicted and sentenced to prison. Do you know how hard it is to sentence the sheriff and the undersheriff of a department as large as the L.A. Sheriff's Department? I mean, the amount of stuff they got away with before being so blatantly criminal that they had to get caught is probably incredible.

Together, those two departments, the LAPD and the LASD, are as large as some armies. The Germans don't have an army that big! And some armies are less violent. These two departments are responsible for policing the majority of L.A. They were in charge of us. But they get to tell the stories about "Black-on-Black crime." So throughout all that time we have corrupt, violent police departments that are running a city. And Los Angeles in the 1980s, the 1990s: it was the wild, wild West. Everybody thought L.A. was *Colors* and all that bullshit, but these motherfuckers were the biggest criminals.

Who are the real "superpredators," you know? What do you call a gang of bad apples? A rotten apple corps? When it's a cop who robs you, you didn't just get jacked—you got *apple jacked*.

In terms of professions, police officers have some of the highest rates of substance abuse and alcoholism. So when a cop kills someone, how come we always hear about the drugs or alcohol in the victim's system, but never about what was in the cop's system? If you're a bus driver who crashes a bus, what happens to you? You get tested for drugs and alcohol right after the crash. If a pilot crashes his plane, what happens? He gets tested. Why aren't police tested the minute something happens?

We keep testing the fucking bus passengers and not the drivers! The minute there's a shooting, the minute there's an ass-whooping caught on video, they ought to be testing cops. How many are on drugs or steroids? We see cops acting irrationally and out of control over and over and yet they're never tested. If I get pulled over and I'm acting erratically or violently, they're gonna ask me if I'm on something. And yet, we see cops throwing little girls to the ground at these protests, beating on people violently for no reason, and fucking shooting and killing people; still, no drug testing.

And why should we pretend that the police are color-blind when the evidence is all around us that they're not? Nobody's gonna thank you for defending the police. You're still subject to racist cops like anybody.

In June 2020, this young Black dude, Jonathan Price, wrote up a long Facebook post about how he thought cops weren't racist: "I've never got that kind of ENERGY from the po-po . . . Not saying Black lives don't matter, but don't forget about your own, or your experiences through growth / 'waking up'." Only a few months later, he was at a gas station in Wolfe City, Texas, and he broke up a fight between two people. Everything was calm, and by the time a cop rolled up, the fight was over. Price felt like he had no reason to fear the police. But this police officer rolled up on him and tased him immediately. He started convulsing.

And then the cop shot him because he "perceived a threat." The Texas Rangers arrested the cop for murder a few days later.

So even a fan of the police got killed by the cops because of the color of his skin.

BLACK LIVES MATTER NOW

Why has it been so hard for some white people to say "Black lives matter"? Still, at this point, after George Floyd and Breonna Taylor, after Daniel Prude and Ahmaud Arbery, after Trayvon Martin and Charlottesville, why is it that some people still won't acknowledge that America doesn't treat Black lives as important?

Why are we set aside, discounted, mitigated, and treated as beside the point? Consider the richness we bring to the American culture, the political movements that we've been at the forefront of, the joy we've brought to the American people with our music, our TV shows, our athletes. And yet too many of our lives are thrown away. If COVID-19 disproportionately kills Black people, maybe it's not a problem. If drugs are a Black problem, maybe it's not a problem. If the economy is a problem for Black people, maybe it's not a problem. Black lives and Black problems are pre–disposed of.

It's only when COVID starts killing white people or when the opioid crisis hits white people or when white people are being evicted that America snaps to attention and gets serious.

Why are white people marching now, when they didn't before?

I think it was primarily because everyone was home and there's only so many episodes of *Tiger King* you can watch. Who knew that a bad case of cabin fever was all it took to get white folks off their asses to support Black lives? That's all we had to do? It took a staycation for our lives to matter?

But all of a sudden, after George Floyd, people went, "Oh, it's wrong to kill Black people," because they ran out of TV to watch. Good thing *Game of Thrones* was over.

But it wasn't just *people* stepping up. I gotta say it was pretty inspiring to see all the corporations step up and embrace the Black Lives Matter movement. Some people think that corporations are heartless, but I ask you: If a corporation can have a change of heart, was it ever really heartless?

I mean, when the Washington Redskins—now known

as the Washington Football Team—tweeted out their support for #BlackoutTuesday, you might have been tempted to feel like it's hypocritical of a team with a racist name to support a movement against racism. Sure, that is one way to look at it.

And okay, maybe Mike Bloomberg's statement on behalf of Bloomberg L.P. that "we must stand together in our condemnation of all bias and discrimination" doesn't totally make up for his stop-and-frisk policy, which targeted the Black community with bias and discrimination.

And sure, you might feel that David M. Solomon, the CEO of Goldman Sachs, stating that "there is no place at Goldman Sachs for racism or discrimination against any group in any form" and that "this is not a time to be silent" is maybe too little too late for a company that profited handsomely from betting against the subprime mortgage racket that stole property from so many Black families.

I mean, corporations get a bad reputation as being profit-driven, amoral, and tone-deaf. But doesn't it make you feel good that Citibank posted that "we must continue to speak up and speak out whenever we witness hatred, racism or injustice"? Okay, yes it's true that, as Judd Legum pointed out in his Popular Information newsletter, Citibank has donated $242,000 to seventy-four members of Congress who were graded F by the NAACP. And sure, the company's corporate PAC donated $180,000 to fifty-three members of the House rated F. And that's just in the House; it doesn't cover donations to senators with F grades.

But don't get mad at Citibank for being hypocritical. Because if you do, you also have to get mad at Google, Amazon, and others who have donated to politicians with F grades too. If you think Citibank is insincere, then you'd also have to believe that Bloomberg, Facebook, the NFL, Reddit, Nike, and Fox are hypocritical. And that's just not a world I want to live in.

WHITE RIOTS

But don't worry, white people got tired of protesting and especially got tired of how all these peaceful protests suddenly became "violent riots." Trump and his allies never waste an opportunity to paint Black people as violent, even when it ain't Black people. I didn't know that Portland, Oregon—a favorite target of worry over violent protests—was so full of Black people.

Former attorney general Bill Barr said about the Black

Lives Matter movement: "That's why these so-called Black Lives Matter people—now that, as a proposition, who can quarrel with the proposition that Black lives matter? But they're not interested in Black lives. They're interested in props: a small number of Blacks who were killed by police during conflict with police, usually less than a dozen a year, who they can use as props to achieve a much broader political agenda. . . . And most deaths in the inner city of young Black males below the age of forty-four, the leading cause of death is being shot by another Black person."

Attorney General Bill Barr said that there aren't a lot of police killings of Black people because less than a dozen unarmed Black people were killed by cops last year. Even if that number were right, to those dozen people, that's a lot. But we have different math.

According to the *Washington Post,* 250 Black people were shot and killed by the police in 2019, just a little over a dozen. And even though Black people make up only 13 percent of the U.S. population, they're still shot and killed by police at twice the rate of white people.

The Blue Lives Matter crowd likes to point out that more white people get shot and killed by police than Black people. But that's because there's way more white people in America. So you have to look at the *rate* of killings. But defenders of cops know this. They're not having a serious argument; they're out to blame Black people no matter what the data says.

And of course Barr didn't want to discuss police shootings or justice for victims of police violence. What he wanted to do was talk about "Black-on-Black crime." Republicans love to express concern over "Black-on-Black crime." Bill Barr wasn't talking about "Black-on-Black crime" because he was worried about Black people. He wasn't concerned for our health and safety, because if he were, he'd show it in one of a million other ways. Talking about "Black on Black crime" is just a way to talk to white people, to *pretend* like he cares about Black people while also dog-whistling that *Black people are violent*.

The notion of "Black-on-Black crime" didn't really take off until the 1970s. At that point, people in the Black community were rightly pointing out that white officials were ignoring Black victims of crime in Black neighborhoods. Warner Saunders, a columnist for the *Chicago Daily Defender*, interviewed a pimp about Black-on-Black crime, who put it this way: "Look, Mr. Saunders, cats like me ain't Black, white, green or any color; we are businessmen. We go where the business is and where the man ain't looking. Can you see me going up to Deerfield, Black as I am, trying to stick up. The man would be on me so fast I couldn't get a chewin' gum wrapper. Out here the man is too busy whooping them Panthers and giving tickets to mess with me. Any way he don't care if niggers get ripped off. But you can bet he's watching his 'thang' back in his own 'hood." Now, that is some serious seventies talk!

So "Black-on-Black crime" is just *crime with people near you,* the result of housing discrimination, poverty, and segregation. It's a misnomer. But by the eighties that catchy title stuck, and pretty soon even the NAACP took it and ran with it. And it became a justification for a whole host of things. But mainly it became a defense for fearing Black people and treating them as if they were somehow more violent than anyone else. The *Chicago Tribune* ran a series of articles on the violence of Black youth, and it all fit the growing Reagan-era notion that Black people were at fault for their own problems. As David Wilson, the author of the book *Inventing Black-on-Black Violence,* put it:

"There was no reason to racialize this. It could have been framed as economic or societal-driven crime—why not call it 'oppressed youth–on–oppressed youth' crime, or 'the disenfranchised-on-disenfranchised' crime?"

But that was the impetus for the War on Drugs and the 1994 crime bill and then New York City's stop-and-frisk program. All of these were manifestations of the same kind of presumption of Black people's guilt.

Bill Barr also said, "The left likes to talk about dealing with the root causes, but all their solutions depend on peaceful streets at the end of the day—education, after-school activities, all this stuff depends on peace." But stop-and-frisk is exactly the kind of program people like Barr support—one that does little but harass Black people. Between 2002 and 2012, over Mike Bloomberg's three terms as NYC mayor, more than 5 million people were stopped. In 2009, Black and brown people were more than nine times as likely to be stopped as white people.

Now stop-and-frisk has ended, but police harassment hasn't. A study by the Data Collaborative for Justice at John Jay College found that "there were 5.8 enforcement actions among Black people for every one enforcement action among White people in 2018." Black people are suspect, over and over. We get the *opposite* of the benefit of the doubt.

When white people make mistakes, America bends over backward to protect them and forgive them. Remember Ethan Couch in Texas? He was sixteen when he and his friends stole a couple of cases of beer, then drove his dad's truck and killed four people stopped at the side of the road. He was driving seventy miles per hour in a forty-miles-per-hour zone and was three times over the legal drinking limit at the time. He killed four people, but at trial, the psychologist testified that Couch's wealth and his indulgent parents were to blame for his behavior. He had been given "freedoms no young person should have," like not being punished after he was found a year earlier in a parked pickup truck with an unconscious, undressed fourteen-year-old girl. He also had been cited earlier for possessing and consuming alcohol as a minor. But the psychologist claimed that Couch suffered from "affluenza"—nobody had ever taught him the difference between right and wrong. So instead of going to jail for homicide, Couch got probation at a private rehab center.

Black people don't have affluenza. We have broke-alepsy. That's what we have.

We don't get the deference and excuse-making that white people do. Remember Brock Turner, the Stanford student who was given six months in jail for raping a girl behind a dumpster, instead of the six years prosecutors had asked for? His dad had written a letter saying that a harsh sentence would be a "steep price to pay for 20 minutes of action out his 20 plus years of life." The judge agreed and said that "a prison sentence would have a severe impact on him. I think he will not be a danger to others." With a white dude, all the judge can see is how much "potential" is being lost—that's not what judges see with Black dudes. It pays to be a rich white dude. And it's incredible to me that later this guy became a Supreme Court justice! Oh, wait, I'm thinking of Brett Kavanaugh.

The police bend over backward to blame Black victims for their own injuries and absolve white supremacists. During protests in Kenosha, Wisconsin, after the police shooting of Jacob Blake, a white seventeen-year-old "militia" member shot and killed two protesters. But instead of condemning Kyle Rittenhouse for shooting people, Kenosha police chief Daniel Miskinis blamed the protesters, not the murderer.

"Everybody involved was out after the curfew," Miskinis said at a press conference. "I'm not gonna make a great deal of it but the point is—the curfew's in place to protect. Had persons not been out involved in violation of that, perhaps the situation that unfolded would not have happened."

So it was the protesters' fault that they got shot because they were out after curfew? The gunman was out after curfew too! Why is it so hard for law enforcement to blame a guy toting an AR-15 for his violence? The cops are predisposed to believe that white "militia" members are on their side. A bunch of white guys roll in from out of state with assault rifles and they are somehow on the side of "law and order." Imagine if a bunch of Black dudes rolled in with guns to "protect" the neighborhood.

The police chief continued: "Last night a seventeen-year-old individual from Antioch, Illinois, was involved in the use of firearms to resolve whatever conflict was in place. The result of it was two people are dead."

See? A white guy was "involved in the use of firearms," not murdering people. He was there to "resolve whatever conflict was in place." You know who was trying to resolve a conflict? Jacob Blake. And he was shot in the back by police.

And what are the predictable results of these incidents? Victim-blaming the Black dude who was trying to help and hero-worshipping the white dude who killed people.

So instead of decrying these murders and distancing themselves from this killer, people embraced him and held him up as a hero. Ann Coulter tweeted, "I want him as my president." Well, Trump's killed thousands of people, so maybe then you do like your presidents to be killing people. Maybe then the next logical candidate is a straight-up murderer.

"How shocked are we that seventeen-year-olds with rifles decided they had to maintain order when no one else would?" Tucker Carlson said on his show. He had to maintain order? What were the cops doing there? Who told this kid to illegally obtain a semiautomatic rifle and head across state lines to play soldier? A teenager threatening protesters with a rifle is "maintaining order"? That's the fucking definition of disorder.

His attorney tweeted out, "Kyle Rittenhouse will go

down in American history alongside that brave unknown patriot . . . who fired 'The Shot Heard Round the World.' A Second American Revolution against Tyranny has begun." What kind of crazy nonsense is that? The Minutemen at Concord were fighting the British, not guarding a T-Mobile store.

But the right-wing embraces gun nuts, as long as they are white. They had the gun-toting Mark and Patricia McCloskey speak at the Republican National Convention, even though their only claims to fame are pointing weapons at peaceful protesters and previously smashing a synagogue's honey-producing beehive. Cool people; a shame they were indicted by a grand jury for unlawful use of a weapon and evidence tampering. After their indictment, Mr. McCloskey spoke to the press: "To everybody out there that's thinking about voting for Joe Biden, the Harris-Biden administration, this is a sign of the times of things to come, the government that views its task as protecting criminals from honest citizens, rather than protecting citizens from honest criminals." The *New York Times* reports that he then corrected himself: ". . . protecting honest citizens from criminals."

So when the judge set Kyle Rittenhouse's bail at $2 million, that didn't deter the right wing from getting their hero out of jail. His family raised over $500,000 on a "Christian crowd-sourcing site" after they were booted from GoFundMe. That's a little short of $2 million, but don't worry, the MyPillow guy, Mike Lindell, stepped in with some cash, and so did Ricky Schroder from *Silver Spoons*.

It's pretty fucked up that they got the kid from *Silver Spoons* putting up bail money, but I guess he sold some of his cutlery. Meanwhile, Scott Baio was on Twitter trying to get the election overturned. It's cool that *Joanie Loves Chachi*, but why does Chachi hate Black people? If Tootie from *The Facts of Life* turns on us, I don't know if I can handle it. I mean, you take the good, you take the bad, you take them both and there you have the facts of life . . . but still!

When white people picture violent protesters, they have this image of a bunch of Black people. But the biggest example of people protesting violently was the Civil War. That's *white* people protesting violently. And honestly, that was one *violent* protest.

That is, up until a bunch of Civil War reenactors stormed the Capitol building. Everybody on the right keeps trying to portray Black Lives Matter as a terrorist group, but they never mounted an armed insurrection. They never tried to organize and kidnap the fucking governor of Michigan. Months before the Capitol riot, the FBI and Michigan state authorities arrested thirteen white guys for planning to abduct Governor Gretchen Whitmer. These are the very people that Trump refused to denounce a week before in the debate with Biden.

These are the Proud Boys. These are the white supremacists. These are the militia members. These people want a civil war, they want to dismantle the government, and they want to kill policemen. But somehow we're the threat? Even though you've got dudes like these guys getting arrested by the FBI?

Who's a bigger threat: Black Lives Matter or Donald Trump? He's the one who inspired these terrorists by tweeting, "LIBERATE MICHIGAN." It's not too hard to draw the line between Trump tweeting that, telling the Proud Boys to "stand back and stand by," and the kidnapping plot. The same month that he tweeted "LIBERATE MICHIGAN," heavily armed white protesters took over the Michigan State Capitol building. Some of the state senators wore their bulletproof vests out of fear of being shot.

And guess who was among these armed militiamen? The Null brothers, two of the dudes who were arrested in the kidnapping plot, were there carrying semiautomatic rifles and wearing body armor. And after their arrest, a sheriff who had spoken at the event defended them, saying, "A lot of people are angry with the governor and they want her arrested." Sheriff Dar Leaf added, "In fact, these guys are innocent until proven guilty, so I am not even sure if they had any part in it." It's this same coziness between law enforcement and these white supremacist militias that led to the cops in Kenosha handing out water to Kyle Rittenhouse and letting him walk past them after he shot people.

And the reason that this group even came to the attention of the FBI was that they had been planning to kill some cops. But Black Lives Matter is the threat to police officers?

And the right wing supported him on all of this, right on through the invasion of the Capitol. It shouldn't be any surprise that people were eventually killed. Because for the right wing, white people aren't the violent ones. Even after the FBI arrested this group, Trump went back to Michigan to campaign and kept condemning Governor Whitmer. He joined in as the crowd chanted "Lock her up!" He has no shame. He's always intent on whipping up more violence against his opponents.

It can be hard to tell who the cops are and who the militiamen are. Sheriffs in Michigan have been saying antigovernment stuff, stoked by Trump, throughout the coronavirus crisis. In July, Sheriff John Wilson of Clare County posted on Facebook that state officials should "stay in LANSING, we will do what we will in FREE MICHIGAN!! YUP. I said it. I'm done with unconstitutional b—— from the SWAMP!"

And later, in the lead-up to Election Day, several sheriffs around the state said that they would not enforce a ban on bringing weapons to polling places. Michigan's secretary of state, Jocelyn Benson, enacted the rule to prevent intimidation at the polls. But several different law enforcement agencies decided that they didn't want to uphold the ban. Benzie County sheriff Ted Schendel said, "It's illegal. She doesn't have the authority to make laws." And Robert Stevenson, director of the Michigan Association of Chiefs of Police, said, "The secretary of state issued these administrative rules, but in researching the issue, there's nothing in the law that gives police the authority to enforce these rules."

So why is it that these police agencies are working so hard to make sure people can bring their guns to the voting booth?

And it's so funny when people like these guys in Michigan compare what they're going through to slavery. Nat Turner didn't start a revolt because he was told to stay home. Nat Turner revolted because he was tired of seeing people brutalized. But these motherfuckers want to revolt because they can't go to the gym.

WE NEED MORE BLACK-ON-BLACK OTHER STUFF

The implication with "Black-on-Black crime" is that we are inherently flawed, inherently violent, and that we only do bad shit to each other.

I had the privilege of talking to future Vice President Kamala Harris on my radio show. She told me that if a Black child has a Black teacher, they're much more likely to go on to further higher education. And, like I said before, if Black women have a Black doctor during childbirth, they're much more likely to have a successful, healthy birth. And generally, if Black people have Black health care professionals involved, the outcome is better. So why is it that "Black-on-Black crime" is the standard by which we're judged? If I could teach you and I could keep you alive, then how is the notion of "Black-on-Black crime" all we hear about? Let's get credit for Black-on-Black doctoring. How does "Black-on-Black crime" mean we're predisposed to violence, but Black-on-Black teaching not mean we're predisposed to learning?

Most Black CEOs, most Black judges, most Black politicians, most Black doctors come from HBCUs (Historically Black Colleges and Universities), and for many of them, college was the first time they were taught by Black people. A lot of them grew up in suburban areas and the first time they ever had Black teachers to any great degree was at HBCUs. And yet HBCUs populate the highest sphere of the country for Black people. When this book goes on sale, we'll have a Black woman who came from an HBCU in the White House. And VP Kamala Harris is from Oakland, which is wild. They actually *grow* niggas in Oakland. They have a factory that churns out niggas in Oakland.

Black people dealing with Black people improves our outcomes in all kinds of ways. In most instances, Black judges are less inclined to give Black people in front of them harsher sentences, because they believe in our redemption. Black doctors believe us when we say what's wrong. Black teachers believe in our potential. But the only Black-on-Black experience you ever hear about from white America is "Black-on-Black crime."

And who judges us more than judges? It's right there in the name. Judges are supposed to be impartially meting out justice to everyone before them, without regard for race, color, or creed. But we know that the courts have become more and more political; just look at the types of judges that Republicans have jammed through and onto the Supreme Court these last few years. Even though Justice Neil Gorsuch said that "there's no such thing as a Republican judge or a Democratic judge. We just have judges in this country," there's a pretty big difference between Brett Kavanaugh and Sonia Sotomayor. And unfortunately, we're gonna see what a big difference there is between Ruth Bader Ginsburg and Amy Coney Barrett.

It turns out that, if you're Black, having a Republican-appointed judge can be hazardous to your health. A 2018 study by two Harvard professors found that Republican-appointed judges sentence Black defendants to three more months than Black defendants would typically get with a Democratic-appointed judge. They also sentenced men to two more months than women. So if you're a Black dude before a Republican judge, you're doubly screwed.

That's not to say you're in the clear if you have a Democratic judge. Because overall, Black people are still sentenced to longer sentences than those of other races who are sentenced for the same crime.

Not every case that comes before judges is going to result in prison time, but that doesn't mean that it's not important. The race of a judge and the race of a litigant can also have an impact on civil cases. One recent study showed that, no surprise, white federal judges were four times more likely to dismiss race discrimination cases than Black judges. And they are half as likely as Black judges to rule in favor of people alleging racial harassment in the workplace.

Criminal cases are a little trickier. A Florida study showed that white judges were harsher on Black defendants than Black judges were. But a study in Louisiana showed that judges gave people of their own race longer sentences. One theory to explain that was that victims of crime might also be Black, so the judges might be more sympathetic to the victim than the perpetrator of the crime. But even though judges have a professional *duty* to be fair, they are at least as likely as normal citizens to display implicit bias. When there are many more white judges and many more Black defendants, the result is that bias translates to harsher sentences and less justice.

So yeah, I don't know, I still think I'd rather have a Black judge. I'm just saying, if I could choose—a Black judge would just make me more comfortable. I don't want to prejudge a judge, but I'd rather go before Judge Joe Brown than Judge Brett Kavanaugh.

I had a conversation on my show with Representative Ro Khanna, the congressman from California's Seventeenth District, which includes Silicon Valley. His constituents are Apple and Zoom and Facebook. All the big tech companies. And what we talked about is that even though

Black people set the trends, even in technology, we never get to participate in the wealth-making mechanisms.

Half the value of the NASDAQ 100 is made up of just six tech companies: Apple, Microsoft, Amazon, Alphabet (Google), Facebook, and Tesla. But big tech companies still have far fewer Black people working for them than other industries. White men are the financiers, and Asians and Indians are the engineers, but where are the Black people?

Back in 2014, a bunch of tech companies pledged to improve their diversity and inclusion. They published reports, pledged money and resources, but hardly anything has changed. Mark Zuckerberg wrote a post in the wake of the 2020 BLM protests saying that "Facebook needs to do more to support equality and safety for the Black community through our platforms," but in five years Black employees had gone from 3 percent of workers to 3.8 percent. Apple's statistics are better—9 percent Black—but most of those employees are not in leadership roles. So we got to make Apple cool when they bought Beats by Dre, but the best we get is to work in an Apple Store.

Alphabet, Apple, Facebook, Microsoft, and Twitter all had small increases in their percentage of Black employ-ces. Amazon did better, but mostly because they counted warehouse and delivery workers. All of these companies were built with mostly white employees, so to increase their percentage of Black workers, they need to be aggressive in hiring and retaining employees. But besides publishing reports about it, what is the incentive to do it?

As part of the conversation around the Black Lives Matter movement, a lot of attention was paid to the fact that there are hardly any Black CEOs in America. The Fortune 500 only has four Black men and no Black women as CEOs.

The CEO of Wells Fargo, Charles Scharf, said that the reason the bank had trouble meeting diversity goals was that there's not a deep bench of qualified Black applicants. "While it might sound like an excuse, the unfortunate reality is that there is a very limited pool of Black talent to recruit from," he said. Wells Fargo employees opened up 3.5 million fake accounts without getting customers' permission so that they could inflate their sales commissions and meet aggressive targets that encouraged fraud. So there's not enough available Black people to hire, but there are enough available Black people to exploit and defraud.

In September 2020, the *New York Times* published an overview of the 922 "most powerful people in America"; business leaders, heads of government, and so on. It found that 80 percent of those people were white, even though 40 percent of Americans are people of color. Of the people it profiled:

- Twenty-four people ran the Trump administration. Three were Asian, Black, or Hispanic. And that's calling Ben Carson Black.
- On the Supreme Court, only two were Black or Hispanic. And that includes Clarence Thomas.
- Among military leaders, only one member of the Joint Chiefs of Staff was Black.
- Only 9 U.S. senators of 100 were Asian, Black, or Hispanic. Only 3 out of 50 governors were people of color, and none of those were Black. Of 431 representatives in the House, 112 were people of color.
- Of the top twenty-five universities, only one was led by a person of color.
- Only three Black or Hispanic people led major news organizations. All five people running book

publishing companies were white and the top ten magazine heads were all white.

In entertainment and sports, it wasn't any better: 2 out of 14 music industry heads, 3 out of 25 TV and studio heads, and 6 out of 99 professional baseball, basketball, and football team owners were people of color.

There it is in black and white: Black people are still not in power because white people are still running the show. They're running all the shows.

And then when companies came under pressure and actually did announce efforts to diversify their workforce, the Trump administration tried to shut them down, claiming they might "violate civil rights laws."

Both Wells Fargo and Microsoft received inquiries from the Department of Labor's Office of Federal Contract Compliance Programs about their diversity plans. Both companies had set out goals to double their numbers of Black senior managers within five years. So an office that normally enforces affirmative action for federal contractors was now being used by the Trump administration to scare companies away from trying to diversify.

Microsoft had to pay a $3 million settlement to the Department of Labor for discriminatory hiring practices just a few weeks before this investigation. So you get sued for discrimination and then investigated for not discriminating? Microsoft can't win. Is Microsoft Black? People hated Clippy so much, maybe he was!

PART V

THE END OF TWO THREATS?

THE BEGINNING OF THE END

As I'm writing this, in December 2020, we have the end of at least two of the biggest threats to Black people in sight: Trump and COVID. If Black people are going to survive America, the end of these two is good news. In fact, the story of the 2020 election is that Black folks saved themselves—and the nation. All the stuff I wrote about in the previous pages drove Black and brown communities to the polls. Our lives were on the line. The ballot was our prescription. But it's worth looking closely at how f-ed up this election was, and how difficult they made it for minorities to exercise their rights. Because I truly believe that the fight for voting rights is a fight for survival.

On December 14, 2020, we had two historic events happen: the Electoral College confirmed Biden's win, and Sandra Lindsay, a Black nurse at a hospital in Queens, became the first American to receive a COVID vaccine.

And on January 6, 2021, we had another one: the armed invasion of the U.S. Capitol by white terrorists, at the direction of President Trump.

Part of the problem of writing a book in the middle of a global pandemic is that I don't know what the world will look like when you get this book in your hands. Maybe you'll be in a postapocalyptic bunker, fighting with other survivors over a can of creamed corn, and have no time to read books. Or maybe you'll all be vaccinated, too busy having "breathe on each other" parties to read books.

It's hard to know the future, but it's also hard to keep hold on the past. Our sense of time has been a victim of this pandemic. Some days have seemed like they wore on and on and others passed by fast. As days blend together, sometimes it's hard to remember whether it's October in Dallas or July in Los Angeles.

But it's important to remember what happened, as it happened. I'm finishing this book up at the beginning of 2021. And I think we'll all remember that the coronavirus outbreak started to uproot our lives in March 2020. We'll all remember how Trump didn't do anything about it except deny it, and then once he got COVID, he *still* didn't do anything about it. We'll all remember how Joe Biden beat Trump, but that Trump denied that too. And at the end of 2020, several vaccines were announced. So it looks like (hopefully) we'll be rid of Trump soon and maybe COVID too.

But if this is all irrelevant by the time you read the book, I hope you'll at least be able to burn it for warmth or cooking beans if you're trapped in a bunker somewhere. Or if you're at a party, it should still make a nice coaster for your drink. Have fun while you can; we all gotta do that, at least.

And as I finished writing up this book, America was also writing up its final chapter with Donald Trump. The stakes were high in this election. If America endorsed another four years of Trump, where would we be? A Joe Biden win wouldn't mean that racism in America was solved, but it wouldn't be the endorsement of the oppression of Black and brown people that a Trump win would be.

In the lead-up to the election, we were in a dangerous moment. For Black people and for America.

BLAMED FOR PRE-LOSING

I always expect Trump and the Republicans to blame Black people for everything, but do you remember how white liberals preemptively blamed us for losing the election?

During the primaries, Bernie was killing it, getting all the votes and enthusiasm. He looked like he was gonna win Iowa and he got New Hampshire and Nevada. Joe Biden didn't have any money or any support.

And then they got to where Black people are. Biden won South Carolina. And then he won Michigan and Texas. Basically, after he got where niggas were, he won. Personally, I knew Bernie didn't have a chance of winning. I knew that his numbers were artificially inflated, because there ain't no niggas in Iowa or New Hampshire.

And liberals were giving Black people shit about it. "Oh, they don't know what they're doing. Bernie's the one! Biden can't beat Trump." All these liberals were so sure of it. Bill Maher said, "But I tell you why Bernie Sanders is attractive to me now: because he's the only Democrat who, like Trump, has an army. Who when it gets to this other level, he's got a bunch of badass motherfuckers who will get in the streets." People like Bill were always arguing that you can't pick an old candidate, you can't pick a candidate who's part of the system, all that kind of stuff.

And then once Biden was the nominee, they were so pissed off. Glenn Greenwald tweeted, "The Democratic establishment—given the choice—would rather lose with Biden than win with Bernie." And take activist Ryan Knight: "Biden will lose to Trump. He doesn't have the energy, vision, or movement to win a national election. Turn off corporate media, get out of your bubble, and go out and talk to the working people of this country. You'll thank me." It's interesting to me that someone with the Twitter handle "@ProudSocialist" thinks he knows more about the working people of the country than Black people do. Black and brown people *are* the motherfucking working people of the country. But progressives were talking to Black people like we had done the worst thing in the world. We didn't know what we were doing. We were talked to like we were pets or children. *Bad Black people! Bad! Now look at the mess you made! Bad!*

But I'm gonna tell you, the people of America don't want to make a change midstride. So, if they have a choice between an unproven commodity or someone familiar, they'd rather stay with the thing they know. Bernie seemed risky. I don't think most Americans had the same response to Bernie that the Bernie Bros did. I think most people knew that Biden was a solid dude, had seen what he had done before, and were going to go with something they knew.

And for Black people, Bernie never would have earned the support that Biden got. Bernie *literally* had a heart attack during the campaign. Really had one; not the made-up shit that was being thrown at Biden. If he had been the nominee, do you know what they would have done to a dude like that, who had a damn heart attack in the middle of the campaign, and who's a socialist to boot? C'mon now.

So while progressives were busy blaming Black people like we always get blamed, telling us that we blew another election, what we were actually doing was saving the country. And, okay, Bernie won California. That was it. He didn't win Texas. He didn't win Michigan. He didn't win nothing else. After that, Black people were like, "We are not voting for this dude who looks like he combs his hair with a balloon. It ain't gonna fucking happen." Even when we're out there saving the country, we never get the credit, always the blame. But we were right! Biden was the winning choice. We had our eyes squarely on the prize: beating Donald Trump in the general election. It was an educated decision; after all, Black people have been studying white folks for four hundred years. We gamed out that Biden had the best chance of beating Trump, so he's the horse we backed.

It's very hard to beat an incumbent president, who has the pomp and circumstance of the presidency behind him and the power of government at his disposal, particularly this one. Because Trump was unscrupulous. Somebody like that, somebody so unscrupulous, who has no morals, who will do anything to win? You need someone steady to beat a guy like that.

Biden's our dude. Because here's the thing: He worked under a Black man and never tried to shit on him. He never tried to belittle him. That shouldn't be unusual, but it is. He never once tried to shit on him. He did his job and he did it well. He looked like he was pleased to be with Obama. He didn't look like he thought it was beneath him. But even liberals were like, "You dumb niggers. I can't believe that you guys fucked this up and it's your fault." So if it's our fault for making sure he was the candidate, do we get the credit for him winning? Of course not.

And meanwhile, COVID had broken out in several big cities. By the end of March 2020, there were over one thousand deaths and eighty thousand cases. By April, 10 million people were unemployed. By the end of May, one hundred thousand Americans had died of the virus. In June, Trump held an indoor rally in Tulsa that killed his pal Herman Cain.

THE PRESIDENT IS SICK

By the time of the first debate between Biden and Trump in September, there had been 7 million cases of COVID-19 in the United States, but what Trump wanted to talk about was Hunter Biden. This was the debate where Trump told the Proud Boys to "stand back and stand by." He was even more unhinged than usual, and little did we know—he was COVID-positive! A few days later, he was being rushed to Walter Reed.

But when Trump got COVID, he didn't come out saying, "Oh whoops, I learned my lesson." No, he came out pretending he was all better, that COVID was no big deal. Instead he downplayed it: "Don't let it dominate. Don't let it take over your lives. Don't let that happen." So if you die from COVID, I guess it's your own fault for letting it dominate you.

Don't let it dominate. This is from a dude who paid $750

in federal taxes, so his tax money wouldn't even pay for the aspirin on a normal person's medical bill. But when Donald Trump got COVID, he had the finest medical attention on the face of the earth. He got around-the-clock care. He had experimental medication. Poor Black people don't have experimental medication. When we get deathly ill, we have our grandmother's Prayer Warriors. That's all we have. All we have is old broads on Facebook praying for us. It's Earline and them with olive oil.

It may not be as good as remdesivir or whatever, but that's what we got. It's Big Mama's Prayer Warriors. We don't get the top medical consultation, we get *"We're standing in the gap, Lord!"* And that's it.

We may never know how many people Trump infected in his own White House by ignoring his health advisers. During the outbreak in the White House, Surgeon General Jerome Adams himself probably should have been quarantined. 'Cause why? Was he "predisposed"? The nigga who started all of this conversation: Was he predisposed to catch COVID, or was he just around worthless white men?

So when *we* die of COVID, it's our own fault for not following "the rules." But white men never follow the rules.

Look at all these white men saying they don't have to wear masks. They hardly ever follow the rules because the rules are not meant for them.

Watching the vice presidential debate, you saw it: Pence could talk over his opponent, interrupt, and ignore the questions, but Kamala Harris couldn't. If she got too vocal or interrupted too much, watch how she'd get criticized. Trump called her a "monster." Trump's first debate versus Biden was out of control, and Pence obviously had a different M.O. than Trump, but the motivation was the same: "Fuck your rules, I'm not listening to you. I do what I want." One just does it a little more bombastically than the other.

And what's the result of all this exceptionalism? Trump didn't have to follow the rules, and he got COVID. Across America, red states are having waves of COVID cases because they won't follow the rules. That's *white people,* by and large. But look at the NBA: They successfully resumed their season in the "bubble" and had no new COVID cases. None. They all went into a bubble because they understood the contours of this disease and its nuances and they listened to the science. They didn't just do what they *wanted*. They acted like grown-ups. They balanced the fact that they needed to make money with the need for safety. And the result was that the NBA had no cases of COVID in the bubble, while the White House had dozens. It's crazy that a place where niggas work is safer than the White House.

It'd be one thing if the White House only had one outbreak. You'd think that after the president himself got it, they'd tighten things up a bit. But no.

At Amy Coney Barrett's confirmation party, at least twelve people got COVID. There might have been more, but we'll probably never know, because they didn't really want to know how many people they infected. Senator Mike Lee, Senator Thom Tillis, Kellyanne Conway, the president of Notre Dame, Trump himself, Melania, Hope Hicks, RNC chairwoman Ronna McDaniel, campaign manager Bill Stepien, and Chris Christie all tested positive after being at the party. You know when you get an invite to a Trump White House party, it might be BYOB: bring your own body bag.

And their first superspreader event was so much fun that they decided to have another one at an Election Night party. Every time I see somebody from the Trump administration, they have COVID. White House chief of staff Mark Meadows, Corey Lewandowski, David Bossie, and

Ben Carson all tested positive after the party. I guess maybe Dr. Carson forgot to wash his healing hands.

Are these people trying to kill themselves so they don't get indicted? You gotta try hard to be this stupid. When you lose an election, you have to leave your office, but you don't have to leave it on a gurney!

And when Trump got better, first thing he did was go out on a balcony, whip off his mask, and start holding rallies again. I mean, you know the man is contagious, so who the fuck is gonna show up to a rally after that?

Normally, there's never more than five Black people at a Trump rally, but somehow that day there were a few hundred. That's because Candace Owens paid her BLEXIT supporters to head over to the South Lawn after a previous rally, as long as they wore their blue T-shirts. BLEXIT is Owens's group that's trying to get Black people to "leave the Democratic plantation." So, no, it's not George Soros paying antifa, it's Candace Owens paying Black people to come to a Trump rally.

Of course the first people they choose to be around this dude is niggas. You don't see nobody who wants to be around him, so of course the first people he has around while he's toxic is niggas. It's unbelievable. And after they meet on the lawn, they have to cut it. A bunch of niggas standing on the White House lawn with this motherfucker who's COVID-positive. Didn't they see what happened to the last nigga who was around him without a mask: Herman Cain?

Here's a dude who believed some shit that wasn't true, and now he's dead. I don't know how many Black men have risked their reputations and sometimes their lives in the service of defending white people's lies. I mean, Colin Powell did it with the Iraq War and it cost him his reputation. Herman Cain did it in the service of a white dude's lie and it cost him his life. He went to the first big COVID-era Trump rally in Tulsa, indoors, in the middle of a pandemic. "Here's just a few of the #BlackVoicesForTrump at tonight's rally! Having a fantastic time!" he tweeted. All to service Trump's lie that COVID wasn't so bad. And a week later, Cain started feeling sick, and then he was dead. And then what did he get? Nothing. They never mentioned him at the Republican National Convention; nobody even mentioned his name. And to add insult to injury, even after he died, his Twitter account tweeted out: "It looks like the virus is not as deadly as the mainstream media first made it out to be." I mean, if you can't log off of Twitter when you're dead, you've got a serious social media addiction problem.

What's crazy about Trump is that he actually believes that he's not racist. "I'm the least racist person in this room," he said at the final debate with Joe Biden—in front of Kristen Welker, *a Black woman*. And *then* he gets mad about not getting credit for how not-racist he is. And it's hilarious: This dude likes to compare himself to Abraham Lincoln. He keeps saying this, over and over.

In a tweet just days after George Floyd died: "My Admin has done more for the Black Community than any President since Abraham Lincoln."

At the NBC Town Hall event that he did to avoid a second debate: "I have done more for the African American community than any president with the exception of Abraham Lincoln."

And then at that last debate with Joe Biden, he said: "Nobody has done more for the Black community than Donald Trump. And if you look, with the exception of Abraham Lincoln."

There've been twenty-seven presidents between Honest Abe and Dishonest Donald. It's fair to say that a couple of the presidents between Lincoln and Trump did *a little bit* more for Black people than Donald Trump did.

A Short List of How Much More Other Presidents Between Lincoln and Trump Did for Black People

- Andrew Johnson—yeah, he did suck.

- Ulysses S. Grant—used troops to shut down the Ku Klux Klan in South Carolina during Reconstruction.

- Rutherford B. Hayes—a devout abolitionist who defeated attempts to force him to repeal the election laws protecting Black voters.

- James Garfield—advocated for civil rights for Black people and was assassinated six months into his presidency, but probably was still a better dude than Trump.

- Chester A. Arthur tried to strategically support reform movements in the South against conservative white Democrats.

- Grover Cleveland—appointed a Black former New York judge to replace Frederick Douglass as recorder of deeds in Washington. Yeah, it ain't much, but still better than Trump!

- Benjamin Harrison—ordered prosecutions for violations of voting rights in the South and pushed voter protection legislation.

- Grover Cleveland—crazy, that guy became president again. But yeah, he didn't do much for Black people.

- William McKinley—before he was president, he condemned lynching, but as president, he, too, didn't do much for Black people—just like Trump.

- Theodore Roosevelt—was a lot like Trump in that he had friendly dinners with Black people, but also thought that Black people were inferior to white people—so he had dinner with Booker T. Washington, not Kanye.

- William Howard Taft—pretty racist dude.

- Woodrow Wilson—very racist dude, just like Trump.

- Warren G. Harding—spoke out after the Tulsa Race Massacre and supported anti-lynching legislation.

- Calvin Coolidge—spoke at Howard University and supported voting rights.

- Herbert Hoover—honestly, pretty bad for Black people but still not as bad as Trump.

- Franklin D. Roosevelt—had a "Black Cabinet" of advisers on race issues, and his wife, Eleanor, was a badass.

- Harry S. Truman—desegregated the armed forces.

- Dwight D. Eisenhower—enforced *Brown v. Board of Education.*

- John F. Kennedy—opposed George Wallace, federalized the Alabama National Guard to enforce civil rights, and more.

- Lyndon B. Johnson—passed the Voting Rights Act of 1965, the Civil Rights Act of 1964, and the Fair Housing Act.

- Richard M. Nixon—a terrible bigot, he still helped integrate schools and ended discrimination in companies and unions that worked under federal contracts.

- Gerald R. Ford—endorsed civil rights legislation and made even the smallest gestures toward school integration.

- Jimmy Carter—launched the Black College Initiative to give more support to historically Black colleges and universities.

- Ronald Reagan—yeah, he was a racist. Maybe not as much of a racist as Trump, but um, yeah. I guess he did sign an extension of the Voting Rights Act, but that's about all you can say.

- George H. W. Bush—signed the Civil Rights Act, which was a sort of watered-down civil rights bill.

- William J. Clinton—America's first "Black president" before we had a real one, Bill Clinton appointed Black people to high cabinet offices and brought a booming economy to the Black community.

- George W. Bush—appointed Colin Powell and Condi Rice.

- Barack Obama—c'mon, man.

So Trump has done more for Black people than *all* of those dudes? Some of them weren't trying very hard—in fact, most of them weren't—but they still did more for Black people than Trump.

Basically, Trump's claim is that he gave Black people jobs, so he can't be racist. He says that the unemployment rate for Black people during his term was the lowest it's ever been in history, which isn't true; it was zero percent during slavery, and I'm pretty sure they hated niggers.

Later in the final debate, Joe Biden made fun of him. "Abraham Lincoln here is one of the most racist presidents we've had in modern history." Trump got confused by that joke, but just so we're clear, Trump is not Lincoln. Not by a long shot. There are a lot of differences between the two:

- *Lincoln* grew up in a log cabin. *Trump* grew up in Queens.
- *Lincoln* wore a stovepipe hat. *Trump* wore a MAGA hat.
- *Lincoln* was assassinated by a failed actor. *Trump* slept with a porn star and then paid her hush money to cover it up.

- *Lincoln* led the Union through the Civil War. *Trump* was impeached for inciting an insurrection.
- *Lincoln* wrote the Gettysburg Address, one of the most memorable speeches in American history. *Trump* ignored all of his public health officials and got more than four hundred thousand people killed from COVID-19.
- *Lincoln* signed the Emancipation Proclamation, setting the stage for the abolition of slavery. *Trump* caught COVID himself after ignoring all of his public health officials.

So you see: they're a little different. Maybe the only similarity is that they both only served four years. You can thank a Make the Confederacy Great Again nut named John Wilkes Booth for that.

Trump wouldn't be Trump if he didn't try to shift the blame for COVID deaths to someone else, preferably Black people, or at least Democrats.

So it was no surprise when in September 2020, Trump

disavowed all responsibility for COVID deaths in blue states: "If you take the blue states out, we're at a level that I don't think anybody in the world would be at. We're really at a very low level but some of the states—they were blue states, and blue-state managed."

New York, New Jersey, California—all big states—got hit first and hardest because the Trump administration wasn't up to the job. At the time Trump said this, eleven of the top twenty states for COVID deaths were "red states." And as Vox put it, "If you somehow 'take the blue states out' and red states were their own country, they'd still be in the top 20 for Covid-19 deaths worldwide."

Maybe we *should* take the blue states out and see how things go. Because it's the blue states that put up the money that keeps this country running, not the red states. As a matter of fact, you could argue that we wouldn't have a United States of America without the people who foot the bill.

But Trump did get some Black support. Shit got scary. Somehow he got Lil Wayne and Lil Pump and Ice Cube to come out and support him, which is weird because that's my fucking playlist!

Trump lost the stalwarts of the Republican Party, the entire national security apparatus disowned him, but he gained Waka Flocka. He lost former presidents and presidential candidates, but he gained Lil Wayne. So he lost Jimmy Carter, but he got the dude who did *Tha Carter II*.

On Election Day, I was like, "Please, please don't let Peaches and Herb support him. If he gets Latimore, or if this motherfucker gets Lou Rawls . . . all hope is lost." It took time to put that playlist together! People were worried about him getting Pennsylvania; I was worried that he got Summer Jam. As more of these names came out, I was just praying, *Please don't let it be the O'Jays.* I couldn't take it. *If it's Earth, Wind & Fire? Or if that son of a bitch gets ahold of Stevie Wonder? I don't know what the fuck I'll do.*

Ice Cube and me got into it, though. Because Ice Cube sat down with the Trump administration to go over Cube's "Contract with Black America." But it was a fantasy to believe that you could get the Trump administration to do anything for Black people. You've seen Black person after Black person after Black person ruin themselves at the altar of Trump and get nothing in return, and Ice Cube is just the latest one. He came in with his Contract with Black America and he walked out with Trump's "Platinum Plan." The *Platinum Plan*. When I heard that, it was insulting right out of the gate. Why didn't they just call it the *Spinning Rims Plan*?

Why was Trump meeting with Ice Cube? We had a third wave of COVID coming and he's meeting with the dude that gave us three *Fridays*. Defenders of Cube were saying that we need a seat at the table. Okay, but we need the right people at the table. We need people from education, from finance, from medicine. People from prison reform, sociology. People who have done this for a living, not people who made a couple of banging albums. Why is it that Trump would meet with Ice Cube but not with Congress? Why would Trump meet with Ice Cube but not debate Joe Biden? Why is it that when Trump met with Black people, it was always actors, comedians, rappers, and athletes? It's because they are all entertainers and that's what he thought this was: entertainment. *The Platinum Plan*.

Ice Cube's one of my favorite rappers. But to sit down with that man who only uses Black people as a backdrop for photo ops? It's insulting. While Ice Cube was meeting with Trump, did he talk to him about how Trump tried to suppress the Black vote? Did he talk to him about the violent supporters waiting to intimidate people? Did they talk about the Proud Boys and why Trump told them to "stand by"? For Trump, when you got the Proud Boys and *Boyz n the Hood* in the same day—yep, that was a pretty good day.

I called Ice Cube out on this bullshit, told him he was getting used, and he sent me an emoji of a middle finger. Rude. But wasn't he getting used? The same week, Eric Trump sent out a doctored photo of Ice Cube and 50 Cent wearing Trump hats. That's a mistake? These are the people who you're sitting down with, who you're legitimizing. You would think that the dude who did *Anaconda* would know a snake when he sees one.

And this was the way that Jared Kushner defended Trump's policies toward Black people on *Fox & Friends:* "One thing we've seen in a lot of the Black community, which is mostly Democrat, is that President Trump's policies are the policies that can help people break out of the problems that they're complaining about. But he can't want them to be successful more than they want to be successful."

A lot of white people talk like that. I think that's the country at large. *Black people don't want to be successful.* This is from a dude who only got into Harvard because his dad made a $2.5 million donation to the school. And then at twenty-seven years old, he became president of a company and his dad was in jail. Now, see, that's the difference. Like in my family: My father raised a family of four on a janitor's salary and he never went to jail. Never. Not one time. And my father didn't leave me any money. I didn't get an inheritance from my father. What I got was some old clothes and a work ethic. That's what the fuck I got from Charlie.

I mean, if hiring a prostitute to sleep with your brother-in-law so you can videotape it and send it to your sister to make sure she doesn't testify in a grand jury is your definition of "wanting to be successful," then I guess, yeah, I don't want to be that successful. I'll take the lessons I learned from Charlie Hughley over lessons from Charles Kushner any day.

But this notion that we're lazy? When so many people are dying of a virus that your father-in-law let spread across the country? The reason the Black and brown people are dying is because they have to *be places*. The people who are dying right now have to be somewhere. That's why it affects the people it affects. They get COVID because they can't stay at home; they gotta go to that bullshit menial job and put themselves at risk or they'll get fired. Now, what's less lazy than that?

And Jared Kushner is a dude who literally lives off people who he *hopes* don't want better. He's a slumlord. In Baltimore, he owns some of the most deplorable projects in all of the country. To be bad like Kushner, you gotta work at it. It's especially galling to hear it from him because when he joined the Trump administration, he retained ownership in Westminster Management, a part of the Kushner Companies. This company paid him $1.65 million in 2019. He directly lives off the very people he says are lazy. So, "lazy niggas" pay his bills.

And while he and his father-in-law's administration mismanaged the COVID crisis, his company pressed ahead with eviction notices for people who fell behind on rent. The *Washington Post* reported that Jared's company submitted hundreds of eviction fillings against tenants during the pandemic. This is par for the course with Kushner's company; they've been sued before by the Maryland attorney general for collecting illegitimate fees and security deposits. They've been pulling this stuff for years, but during the pandemic it's even more abusive. The CDC issued a moratorium on evictions, but companies like Kushner's still file them, even if they can't collect. They rack up court fees and make sure they keep pressure on tenants' necks. A lot of renters just leave because they are harassed out of their apartments.

People like Kushner play by different rules. At the same time he was trying to evict working people from his apartments because "they don't want success," the Kushner Companies was stiffing other companies for mortgage payments on retail space they had in Manhattan. The pandemic made it hard for them to lease the space at 229 West 43rd Street, so they just didn't make their payment. Huh. Luckily, the only eviction that matters with Kushner is him leaving the White House.

Even if a lot of white people didn't agree with Jared's racist views, the largely positive support for the Black Lives Matter protests had faded by election time. The Black Lives Matter protests still weighed on the minds of voters, but your race again became the deciding factor in how you viewed the protests. If you were Black, the ongoing violence by police was a major factor in supporting Biden. And for most whites, the continual pumping up of "looting" in the right-wing media kept them in Trump's corner. It's not so surprising that such a major event would stay in people's minds as they went to vote, but it's a little surprising *how many* people were still affected by it when they went to the polls. Nine out of ten voters said the protests over police violence were a factor in their voting, according to data from a large voter survey by the Associated Press. But even though the protests were a major factor, the split in these voters was still 53 percent Biden to 43 percent Trump— the protests basically reinforced people's prior ideas about the candidates and their positions.

Liberal activists hoped that the protests would be a galvanizing moment for America, forcing people to confront our racist history. And maybe they did for some people. But moderate Democrats like Virginian congresswoman Abigail Spanberger were busy blaming liberal activists for calling to "defund the police," saying that it cost them votes. Actually, in places like Detroit, turnout among Black voters was much higher than before. So people like Spanberger are ignoring the Black turnout again, pretending like the *right* message for Democrats is the one that appeals to white people and "centrists." But this is a Fox News message, a bit of propaganda aimed at white people to scare them about looting and rioting, even though that happened in a small minority of the protests that occurred.

When researchers looked at the incidents of violence at protests, they found that the protests were overwhelmingly peaceful. And where there was violence, it was usually directed *at* protesters by the police. Without violent cops, a lot of these protests would have no violence.

Now right-wing politicians and media deliberately conflate property damage and personal violence, as if someone throwing a brick through an Urban Outfitters window is as serious as police beating on someone. Taking a pair of Nikes isn't as serious as taking a billy club to the head. But even the Department of Homeland Security's Homeland Threat Assessment referred to "over 100 days of violence and destruction in our cities."

Police were reported injured in only 1 percent of the protests. And less than 4 percent of the protests involved property damage or vandalism. And when violence did start, it was often in reaction to police beginning or escalating it. If you just watched Fox News, you would think that almost all of the protests were violent.

But cops did show some restraint. At least they did if you were in a pro-Trump protest. You wouldn't believe how patient cops were with guys like that.

Right before the election, Trump supporters, in their pickup trucks with their flags flying, stopped in the middle of the Garden State Parkway in New Jersey, and then did it the next day on the Whitestone Bridge in New York. But the cops didn't start busting heads or ramming their cars through protesters like they did before. Remember a few years ago, when conservatives were hyperventilating about Black Lives Matter protesters shutting down highways? *How are ambulances gonna get through? There's blood on your hands!* And so on. But now that it's a pickup truck with a MAGA flag, it's okay?

When a bunch of white people tried to force their way into a Detroit election office to stop votes from being counted, did the cops whoop their asses? Why not?

Trump was banking on his MAGA fans to put him back in office. He didn't care about Black people or blue states or a whole host of other people who hated him, who he was letting die. He just appealed to his core audience again. But you'd think Trump would at least care about all these old people dying of COVID. You'd think he'd care about them. Because a lot of those people are people who voted for Trump, and they won't be able to anymore because they're dead now.

Trump did everything he could to steal the election, including removing mailboxes. But he didn't need to remove mailboxes to win; he needed to remove death certificates. He should have been more careful talking about voter fraud: "Oh, you know they're letting dead people vote. They're putting dead people on the voter rolls." Well, you might need that right now. Those are your constituents. You know the expression "If Grandpa was alive, he would roll over in his grave?" Well, Trump should have hoped that he did—and then headed to the polls.

Turnout was huge. More than 158 million people voted, the largest voter turnout in American history.

I think people were shocked at the high voter turnout in the Black community. And I don't even know how Black people mailed in their ballots, because he stole all the mailboxes. Even without mail-in voting, we had a huge number of early voters. That's how much Black people hate him. We hate him so much we're on time for something.

We hate him so much we're early. We didn't even get out of *slavery* early. Juneteenth is a celebration of Black people not knowing they were free for two years. We weren't even early for emancipation, but we were early to get rid of Trump, goddammit. We got that.

It should be good news that Trump lost the election. But the stark thing about Biden's win is that it showed how many people were still willing to give Trump another shot and sign up for four more years of white supremacy.

Some liberal white folks were surprised that it wasn't a landslide win for Biden. I wasn't. Black folks have been clear-eyed about how racist this country is in a way that white people on the left haven't. To think that there's a silent majority of white voters out there who would rise up to repudiate Trump? We've been disappointed so many times that we can't allow for hope like that. To think that would be to ignore history. To think that would be to ignore the last four years.

The white people who came out for the Black Lives Matter protests were already Biden supporters, and any stray white people who were newly supportive of Black lives mattering had already decided that "looting" and "riots" were a problem by the time the election rolled around. They were back in the fold, willing to give Trump a pass again if it meant they didn't have to wear a mask and they could wish away the coronavirus. Black lives might have mattered in June, but by November? "Freedom" mattered more. Freedom to ignore science—one hundred thousand infections a day on November 3—to do what they wanted, regardless of the consequences for Black and brown people.

And speaking of Black and brown people: Brown people in Georgia bailed us out of this fucking mess, while some "brown" people in Florida tried to keep us in it. NBC News reported that 55 percent of Florida's Cuban Americans voted for Trump. It turns out Cubans don't give a fuck about Mexicans any more than white people do. The so-called Latino vote is kind of an illusion. Talking heads like to come on TV and speak about the "Hispanic vote" like it's some kind of unified voting bloc, when they're really talking about folks of different ethnicities from dozens of different nations and territories. You can't expect a guy from Brazil to have the same concerns as someone from Guatemala, Mexico, or Cuba. I understand that. Still, if you don't think Trump and the Republicans would deport all your brown asses if given half a chance, you're dreaming.

BLAMED FOR WINNING?

Biden picked up a lot of votes from older voters, which traditionally never happens with Democrats. But that wasn't the story. No, the story we kept hearing was that Trump did a lot better with Black people and Latino voters this time around. The story was that he got 20 percent of Black men. This is just another example of how the media goes looking for a way to blame Black people. How is it that *we're* the reason that this race was so close? So in order for Biden to have had a comfortable cushion, we had to come out for Biden at *ninety percent*? Ninety-five percent? You want a hundred percent? Every Black man?

The real story isn't that 20 percent of Black men voted for Trump; it's that 80 percent voted for Biden. It's that 75 percent of Latino men voted for Biden. But 65 percent of white America voted for Trump. The majority of white America voted for a racist psychopath. It isn't us who did this. It's that, knowing what you knew, you still voted for a racist psychopath. What happened to Trump is that he ran out of Cubans and rednecks. The real story isn't that a majority of us voted against a racist psychopath; it is that most of white America voted *for* one. And yet, we keep hearing about Trump and his gains with Black people. Yeah, okay. It ain't hard to believe that a motherfucker like Lil Wayne, who basically *raps* about the shit Trump *does,* would like him. It's just that it isn't Lil Wayne that we should be talking about; it's Ma and Pa Kettle.

Trump increased his voting totals among rural voters, and Biden increased his among people in urban communities. Biden won the majority of the counties that are doing well and want to do well. Trump won the counties that aren't doing so well. That's because the only place for Black people is forward, not backward. We're not buying this "Make America Great *Again*" nonsense. We don't hold a nostalgia for the way things were when we were oppressed, discriminated against, and told we were less than white people. The only place for us is forward. Donald Trump doesn't know it, but Black people don't just live in the inner cities anymore. We live in cities that are connected to the suburbs. So ultimately, we do well when there is a mix of other people; when we live in places with more diversity, we thrive and things are better for us. We don't get to live in homogeneous enclaves like rural white Trump voters. The homogeneous enclaves we get to live in are prisons.

Black people won this election for Biden. Name me one other group that concentrated behind one candidate to the same extent as Black people. You can't get 50 percent of people in America to do anything. But we voted at 75, 80 percent for Biden. Biden didn't win Georgia. He won *Atlanta*. He didn't win Pennsylvania; he won *Philly*. He won Pittsburgh. He didn't win Wisconsin; he won Milwaukee. He didn't win Arizona; he won Phoenix and Tucson. He won where Black and brown people live in large numbers. That's where he won.

If you look at the two biggest stars in the Democratic Party two or three years ago, it was Stacey Abrams in Georgia and Andrew Gillum in Florida. And in the 2018 election, both of them ran these great campaigns, but in the end both of them got cheated. Brian Kemp ran against Stacey Abrams while he was the secretary of state, in charge of counting the votes. And he did some very underhanded shit, and even if he didn't technically break any laws doing it, you can't tell me he didn't steal that election. The same thing to a greater or lesser degree happened to Gillum in Florida.

Now, Andrew Gillum was so devastated by the loss that he got drunk and ended up in a hotel room with a male escort. Stacey Abrams did something different. Staccy Abrams used the loss to motivate her to make things better, to make sure that wouldn't happen again. She made sure that what happened to her would be laid bare for everybody to see so it wouldn't happen again. Seems like Gillum turned to meth and men, and Abrams turned Georgia Democratic. I'm gonna start calling her Ty-D-Bol, because she turns shit blue!

Black women are what delivered Georgia and won Biden his election. So while Trump was out there spreading corona, Stacey Abrams was spreading hope.

Unlike any presidential candidate before, Trump refused to concede his loss. In his mind, and in the minds of his voters, Trump was the winner on Election Day because the Election Day returns were going his way. "I WON THIS ELECTION, BY A LOT!" Trump tweeted. Even on November 10, days after all the major media outlets had called the election for Biden, he tweeted "WE WILL WIN!" So which is it, did he win or will he win?

Trump and the Republicans somehow think it's suspicious to count votes. "We were winning in all the key locations by a lot, actually. And then our number started miraculously getting whittled away in secret," he tweeted. But the reason it seemed suspicious to Trump was because it was happening in places like Philly. They were counting votes where niggas live. And you know what's funny? Republicans trying to cast aspersions, saying "Why is it taking so long to count?" Well, it's taking so long because we get everything last. All you're doing is hearing what we have to say. That's why these votes are taking so long. Because America is finally having to hear what we have to say. Our vote is our vote, and our voice is our voice. So you're going to have to sit there and America is finally being forced to listen to what we have to say.

Republicans tried hard to set this thing up to fail. And when it failed to fail, they just tried to throw dirt. In all the places where counting took a long time, it was set up that way by Republican legislators. In Philly, they weren't allowed to count early votes until Election Day. In Detroit, where a crowd of Trump supporters tried to barge into the room where ballots were being counted, Republicans then complained that people covered up the windows to the room. Inside the room, Republican observers tried to slow down the vote, challenging ballot after ballot. And it's not surprising that the mostly Black crowd of Detroit poll workers was being accosted and challenged by the mostly white Republican poll observers. One Republican election challenger told her colleagues, "Challenge every ballot." That's been their playbook all along, during this whole election. And even after the election.

But it wasn't Black people who failed. We aren't to blame. About 90 percent of Black voters went for Biden. If you put ten Black people in a room, nine of them voted against a racist psychopath. If you put ten white people in a room, six of them voted for him. I mean, what does it take for Black folks to get credit?

You lost. And niggas did it. You lost because most people with melanin in their skin fucking hate you. That's why you lost. Everybody has their weakness. Superman has kryptonite and Trump has Wayne County. America has been sick with Trump, but the antidote to Trump is apparently melanin.

BLACK VOTES MUST BE CORRUPT

Do you know how hard it is to beat an incumbent president? It's hard enough when somebody has the powers of the president that Trump legitimately had, but when that person is also willing to do extraordinary things? When someone's willing to lie and to steal to be president? When someone's willing to do anything? What's crazy is: Trump would do anything to win—except his job. Instead, he'd rather try to claw back the results of a huge loss.

He's not mad because he lost. He's mad because he cheated and lost. And he just knew that with all the cheating he'd done, he couldn't lose.

Bill Barr told the Justice Department that it could investigate voter fraud—a highly unusual interjection into electoral politics. The longtime employee in charge of election fraud crimes stepped down in protest, and sixteen federal prosecutors across the country who monitored elections told Barr that they hadn't found any evidence of fraud.

If you're having the Justice Department investigate voter fraud, shouldn't we start with the fact that the post office was politicized? Shouldn't we investigate how they stole mailboxes and took out sorting machines to deliberately make it harder to vote by mail? I think one of the reasons that voter turnout was so high was that a lot of people thought they weren't gonna get the chance to vote, that people were trying to take their votes away from them. So they moved to mail-in voting. There were over 100 million mail-in ballots and 40 million same-day votes. But that huge early vote is because people thought basically it wasn't gonna happen.

You see, in Trump's mind, the only way he could have lost is if there was "massive voter fraud." But not just any voter fraud: apparently it was only Black voter fraud. It's no mistake that Trump kept trying to pin these election fraud allegations on Philly, Milwaukee, Detroit, and Georgia. Because that's where the Black people are.

In Philly, Trump claimed that the "Philadelphia Commissioner and so-called Republican (RINO), is being used big time by the Fake News Media to explain how honest things were with respect to the Election in Philadelphia. He refuses to look at a mountain of corruption & dishonesty. We win!"

But when Trump's lawyer, the honorable Rudolph Giuliani, argued his case in court, somehow the corrupt judge wasn't persuaded. U.S. District Judge Matthew Brann wrote, "Even assuming that they can establish that their right to vote has been denied, which they cannot, Plaintiffs seek to remedy the denial of their votes by invalidating the votes of millions of others. Rather than requesting that their votes be counted, they seek to discredit scores of other votes, but only for one race. This is simply not how the Constitution works."

In Wisconsin, what galls me is that even with the recounts, Trump didn't want to spend the whole $8 million his campaign would have to pay for a full Wisconsin recount. He only wanted to recount the Black areas. He was gonna go after Milwaukee and Racine only. He was gonna do it a la carte.

In Wayne County, which includes Detroit, the Republican election board members initially refused to certify their county's election results over small inconsistencies, even though they were ready to certify results in other, whiter communities. They wanted to certify everything except Detroit. Those same discrepancies existed in the white suburbs in 2016, but they didn't raise a fuss about that. Biden won 95 percent of the vote in Detroit, and that is why the Republicans tried to block it. Eighty-one million people voted for Biden in this election. Eighty-one million motherfuckers all over the country. How big is that polling place?

How long were those people there? How many people did they see? Even in Michigan, he won by more than 140,000 votes. So Detroit was the center of all the malfeasance?

It was only after Black voters shamed the election board into action that they certified the vote. It isn't even hard to ascribe this to racism; one of the two Republican board members, William Hartmann, had a public Facebook page full of racist memes. And then after certifying the votes, they tried to rescind that certification the next day, apparently after Trump himself called the other Republican board member, Monica Palmer. That there is brazen obstruction by the president. Unfortunately for Trump, the Michigan secretary of state's office ruled that basically there are "no backsies." Ultimately, Trump bet on the wrong Wayne. Biden had Wayne County, Trump had Lil Wayne. One leads you to federal office, and the other leads you to federal charges.

In Georgia, Trump toady Senator Lindsey Graham called the secretary of state, Brad Raffensperger, and tried to get him to throw out ballots from Democratic-leaning counties. Why is a senator from South Carolina calling a secretary of state of Georgia? Oh, he just wanted to learn more about Georgia's signature-matching procedures because he's a fan of penmanship, I guess. Maybe he's training to be a handwriting analyst.

And then the two Republican senatorial candidates who were facing runoffs in Georgia called on Raffensperger to resign. They said that there were "too many failures in Georgia elections this year." The failures were failures to deliver the votes to Republicans, despite the efforts to disenfranchise Black people.

It's the same all over. In each of the states where Trump lost, he targeted the Black areas. All he had to do was go, "You know these niggers . . . You know these Mexicans." Biden won where there's Cesar Chavez Boulevard and he won where there's Martin Luther King Jr. Boulevard. Trump won at casinos. They should've known something was wrong when the blackjack table was empty.

So Trump kept trying to paint these cities where Black people live as corrupt. But as the *New York Times* reported, none of those cities had big surges or changes in voting for Biden. They voted Democratic just like in 2016. The areas outside of those cities are what changed, tipping the election to Biden. But blaming Black people is how Trump always does it. Michigan's attorney general, Dana Nessel, called it out: "Really the themes that we see, that persist, are this: Black people are corrupt, Black people are incompetent and Black people can't be trusted."

So Trump tried to steal the election from people who are only here because they, themselves, were stolen. Trying to disenfranchise Black people's votes is no different from when the Constitution said that we were three-fifths of a person. In the end, no matter how this election was lost, ultimately Donald Trump lost by millions of votes. By over 7 million, actually. And what they told us was because it's niggas and Spanish-speaking people and Indians we're talking about, that they're not quite as American, so they don't count as much. They weren't trying to *recount*. They were trying to *discount* the areas where Black, brown, and American Indian people live. Nothing was about turning over the preponderance of the votes; it was about delegitimizing the *people* who voted. It was saying that somehow, these people weren't really Americans, so why should they have a hand in voting? Because by the sheer number of votes, no recount was gonna tell a different story. Lindsey Graham called the secretary of state in Georgia and tried to get him to not count Black people. The certification board in Wayne County tried to decertify just Detroit— just Black people.

Does this even make sense? As if Black people in the inner cities, who had fewer polling places, shoddy voting equipment, and long lines to vote, somehow perpetrated the greatest voter fraud in history. All this while being suppressed and intimidated and poll-watched. Somehow Black people managed to influence Republican sycophants like Governor Brian Kemp and Secretary of State Brad Raffensperger of Georgia? So you believe that secretaries of state and attorney generals and governors and election officials all across the country, in traditionally Republican states like Arizona and Georgia, with Republican legislatures, were complicit in . . . what?

If it were a spate of bank robberies, then yeah—I can understand how white people would try to say "it must be Black people." But this is voter fraud. Black people don't commit voter fraud. What exorbitant schemes of voter fraud have Black people been involved in? When did we ever commit massive voter fraud? When did that happen? So you can't be suspicious of us because of our long history of voter fraud. Massive three-card monte fraud? Sure. Or massive Nigerian prince Bitcoin fraud, okay, you got us. But voter fraud ain't our thing.

But it is white people's thing. It's always powerful white people's thing. Remember how in 2016, before he knew he won, Trump said that there were buses full of Mexicans coming up who were gonna vote illegally? I guess this time there weren't enough of them. Where were they this time? The bus drivers were all sick, apparently. This time it was Black people.

If the election were rigged, would we rig it this way? Republicans picked up seats in the House and flipped a seat in the Senate, but it's rigged? If it were rigged, we would have gotten rid of Mitch McConnell and Lindsey Graham. If we did rig it like that, I'd be the first to call for an investigation; we'd need to investigate how we're so bad at rigging shit!

And then when Pfizer announced that they had an effective coronavirus vaccine right after the election, Ted Cruz was out there saying, *Oh, big surprise. Now there's a cure for COVID.* So I guess now Pfizer is in a conspiracy with the Biden administration. This is some incredible conspiracy: its tentacles reach to Big Pharma, some Republican secretaries of state (only when calling the presidential race, not the senatorial races), the Republican legislatures of various states (only in certain instances), and election officials in Georgia who were clever enough to make sure that we didn't win outright but had to fight it out in two special elections. Very, very diabolically clever.

Seventy percent of Republicans said that they believe there was massive voter fraud in the election. It's amazing to me that Republicans believe in massive voter fraud despite seeing no evidence—but they don't believe in systemic racism in spite of seeing all kinds of evidence. It's like they believe in the Tooth Fairy, but not a dentist.

The point here is that you don't even have to prove anything. You could say whatever you want about Black people and the MAGA mob will believe it, absent proof. Even the movie *Doubt* was about a nigga, even that. No, you don't have to prove shit. All you have to do is raise doubts, make niggas seem suspicious, crafty, criminal, different. All you have to do is say, well—it's worked for doctors: "They're not like us"; it's worked for prosecutors: "They're violent"; it's worked for banks: "They're a credit risk." It's worked so many times, because you know, they're Black.

Because America is predisposed to see us as devious. It can't just be that these people hated Trump so much that they turned out en masse to vote against him. It had to be these *darkies, these nefarious darkies found a way to niggerate the system.*

How could he have lost? With all these niggers voting in all these cities and standing in line? It had to be fraud. *They had to do something.*

They had to do something to get into this school. They had to do something to get this job. They had to do something to win. They couldn't do it honestly because I set the system up against them. How did they fucking beat it? Ain't no way you could really win unless you cheated. I know what I did to win. Everything we win at, we had to do something wrong to do it. *How'd you get that home? How're you sitting in first class? How'd you get that car? How the fuck did you get in?*

There's nothing you could ever say about Black people that America wouldn't believe, except that they were qualified for a job or that they had a high enough GPA to get into school. That's all they wouldn't believe. Everything else, they believe.

IT AIN'T OVER UNTIL . . . ?

Trump never believes anything good about Black people or anything bad about himself. He got fired by America, but then he wouldn't leave. The man wouldn't concede and just continued to tweet out lies about how he had actually won. On November 16, more than a week after the election had been called for Biden, he still tweeted, "I WON THE ELECTION!"

And instead of finally telling him that enough's enough, Republicans bent over backward to allow him to continue living in this fantasy. Mitch McConnell said, "President Trump is one hundred percent within his rights to look into allegations of irregularities and weigh his legal options." Other people said that Trump just needed more time to adjust to his new reality. But when has Trump ever adjusted to reality?

And look where it got us. He tried to have his supporters overthrow the government. Imagine if a Black man wouldn't leave the White House. What if Obama had said, "Hey I just think I'll stick around a little longer." Do you think anyone would have been worried about hurting his feelings? Would anyone have said, "Give him time . . . You have to understand that this is all very new to him."

Black people are used to getting evicted. I guess this is a first for Trump. He could plead with his landlord (America), but I don't think it'll matter that much. *Look, you've been a problem tenant the whole time. I get nothing but complaints about you. I warned you about not having parties here during a pandemic and then you did it again, bro! And, what the fuck—did you put up that gold chandelier? Who told you that you could put up this giant fence outside? And your wife dug up the fucking garden I planted! Okay, man, that's it, you've gotta go. Plus, I already got a new tenant moving in next month and I've gotta give this place a deep clean before he shows up. This place stinks.*

One thing that I don't like is that when white people get mad about losing, we give them something. Like the Electoral College. We'll give them something because we don't want them to feel bad about losing, because losing is for niggers.

I mean, if you lose the Super Bowl, I don't give a fuck who you are; you still have to get in line and shake somebody's hand and say, "Good game. *You won.*" If you don't shake somebody's hand, you could get fired. If a Black person wouldn't shake somebody's hand, we'd never hear the end of it. A Black person scores a touchdown, he can't even dance in the end zone. But you can sell the country?

Why is it that whenever white people lose, we give them something? We fire some motherfucker from a corporation that he ran into the ground; he gets a golden parachute. Megyn Kelly defended blackface on NBC and they still paid her the last $30 million of her $69 million contract after they fired her. Bill O'Reilly sexually harasses a bunch of women, Fox has to pay them $13 million in a settlement and O'Reilly still walks away with $25 million severance. Roger Ailes sexually harassed women and got $40 million to leave. You know what niggas get when they leave? The door. We get out. That's what we get.

First off, the Constitution was written so a dude like Trump couldn't become president. That was like their main goal. So they fucked that up. I'm not a constitutional scholar, but these motherfuckers must not have known what kinda people we would be. You can't give a disgruntled employee two months before he has to clear out his office! *You're fired, you've got two months to finish things up.* Do you know the shit I would do to my job if I got fired and still had two months to fuck shit up? Are you crazy? I'd sell California.

And this guy's crazier than I am. In the last weeks of his

presidency, this motherfucker's selling weapons to people in Saudi Arabia; he's saying it's okay to dump toxins in the water. I thought he'd probably pardon himself or put his face on the dollar bill. I mean, come on man. I knew that this guy was gonna lose and fuck shit up in a way that no Black man could get away with.

But even I didn't expect him to tell a mob of supporters to storm the Capitol. I mean, even with months of threats and encouraging violence, lying about voter fraud, and saying that the election was stolen, even I was a bit surprised.

And it was a shock to see the diversity in the crowd! You had a broad coalition of white people busting through windows, smashing down doors, and ransacking the offices: Not just white supremacist Proud Boys but also QAnon supporters in animal skins. The crowd ran the gamut from white militia members of the Oath Keepers to white militia members of the Three Percenters. And it was a family event: one of the dudes who entered the House chambers in full tactical gear even brought his mom.

But where were the cops? There were hardly any cops around the Capitol building, even as the crowd grew more violent. I've never noticed a shortage of police officers when a nigga gets pulled over for a traffic stop. Matter of fact, I think that all the police must have left the Capitol to swarm around some Black dude with his taillight out.

Because how else do you explain the discrepancy between the police response at the Capitol and the police response we got accustomed to seeing earlier in the spring? When this mob of white rioters broke windows and smashed their way into the Capitol, did the police beat them like they did Black demonstrators during the George Floyd protests? When they chanted "Hang Mike Pence," did the police club them like they did people chanting "No Justice, No Peace?" Why this newfound restraint?

By and large, it's because these were their people. These rioters, these terrorists, were their friends and neighbors. White faces yelling for white power wasn't cause for alarm. It's weird that policemen feel more compassion for a white terrorist than they do for a Black motorist. And as this investigation goes on, we'll find out more about how many police officers were in on it. A number of Capitol police officers are under investigation and officers from more than a dozen other police departments around the country have been identified as attending the rally and storming the

Capitol. So now America truly knows what it's like to be terrorized by the people who are supposed to protect you.

So much attention has been paid to the death of Ashli Babbitt, the white terrorist who was shot trying to vault her way into the Speaker's Lobby. We get to read all about her Air Force service, her troubled life afterward. People want to understand her and hear her brother explain to the *New York Times* that "If you feel like you gave the majority of your life to your country and you're not being listened to, that is a hard pill to swallow. That's why she was upset."

It says a lot about America that more white people are grieving the death of a white woman killed while perpetrating a terrorist attack than they grieved a Black woman killed in her bed.

At the end of Trump's time in office, COVID took off in all the red states, in all the rural areas that nevertheless supported Trump. One stark case was Louisiana, which had a big problem in Black areas early on, like New Orleans. But now, it's disproportionately affecting white people, and it's because they won't wear masks. You would think that people in a state that famously wear hoods wouldn't have a problem wearing masks. But they do. I mean, hell—it'd be easy. Just go in the closet and retrofit some of those hoods. Just cut the point off the top and you're halfway there.

The reason that this disease is so insidious in America is because it preys on selfishness. It preys on the selfishness of people who just want to do what they want, regardless of the harm. It preys on people who have no choice but to be at work around people who won't wear masks. Wearing a mask is an act of compassion, and that's in short supply in America. White people are too busy blaming Black and brown people to blame themselves. COVID is fueled by selfishness.

COVID required America to come together at the moment we were least able to do that. Why would a MAGA-hat-wearing Trump supporter wear a mask to protect a Black girl working at the grocery store? "Freedom" is more important to that dude. That's why you see videos of old white dudes shoving workers at Walmart when they're asked to wear a mask. Making a small sacrifice to protect others isn't something they're interested in. They understand what the scientists say, they just don't spark to it. They don't respond to it.

■ ■ ■

But at the end of it all, Donald Trump lost to a ticket with a Black woman on it. He couldn't stand that. He couldn't take it. And neither could his supporters. Like a body fighting a fever, it took an armed insurrection to finally get people to see how sick America is.

So it looks like Trump is one for the history books. I mean this motherfucker got impeached more than he got elected. He did something no other president's ever done! He's one and two.

Two of the biggest threats to our survival are on their way out. I hope that Trump getting tossed to the curb is the end of it. Unfortunately, even though Trump is gone, Trumpers remain. Maybe by the time you read this book Donald Trump will be a distant memory. But the MAGA crowd is still out there; the Junior Trumps like Josh Hawley and Matt Gaetz and, of course, Don Jr. still want to maintain white supremacy and blame Black and brown people for their own problems. Feeling aggrieved and casting blame on others, especially *the scary Black people,* is just how they do.

And the vaccine is being rolled out, but we'll have to see

if the same systems of inequity make its distribution un-fair. Black and brown people have been disproportionately harmed by the virus, so will the Biden administration be able to get the vaccine to the people who need it most? Can he get the community to trust a medical establishment that hasn't earned our trust?

So far, the news is not good. As of February 2021, the disparities in distribution are already clear. Here in L.A., less than 4 percent of vaccine doses have gone to Black residents. And at the peak of our winter wave of infections, paramedics were told that they could refuse to bring COVID patients to the hospital. They were told that if it didn't look like a patient was going to make it, they could decide not to take them. Isn't that the way it's always been for Black people? *They're not gonna make it,* so why put money into their schools? *They're not gonna make it,* so why bring businesses to their neighborhoods? *They're not gonna make it,* so why save their lives?

COVID hasn't changed things; it's just crystalizing what we already knew.

CONCLUSION

THERE'S NO VACCINE
FOR RACISM

So I don't think that it's our fault that Black people are where we are, even though America has tried to blame us.

The past four years, and especially this last year, have been a stress test for the United States. I've got preliminary test results back, and America, there's some good news and some bad news. The bad news is that I've identified some very serious underlying conditions that could kill you at any time: racism, mostly. And the underlying belief of white people that Black people are the cause of their own troubles, that we're predisposed toward violence and ruin. One very serious malignant cancer—President Trump— was removed, but even though we're in remission, there's still a chance of it recurring, in 2024 or before. And cancerous cells like Donald Trump Jr., Mitch McConnell, and Lindsey Graham are still circulating in our system. And you tested positive for coronavirus.

And let's say we could solve all of these problems. Let's say COVID goes away and we lock Trump up. Let's say in the future, America gives us jobs and makes sure the police are accountable and makes sure we have health care. In short, let's say we're allowed to survive America—then what? Because I think that our mothers' and fathers' mission was never for anything more than that; their mission was for us to survive. Their goal was for us to survive, not thrive. They taught us how to not die; they didn't teach us how to live. That's our big challenge in the next years.

The good news? I think we're gonna survive America, despite it all. All of the underlying conditions remain, however, and the only course of treatment I prescribe is for America to start being fair to Black people. Until that time, I can only point out the problems and hope that seeing clearly will cause America to change. There's no vaccine for racism.

Okay, thanks for coming in today—the nurse will see you on the way out. Do you want a lollipop?

ACKNOWLEDGMENTS

Once again, I want to thank my literary crew: my editor Peter Hubbard, my collaborator Doug Moe, and my agent Richard Abate. I'm grateful for my radio family: David Kantor, Skip Cheatham, and Jasmine Sanders. Thanks to Leyna Santos; Yvette Shearer; my Comedy Get Down brothers, Eddie Griffin, Cedric "The Entertainer," and George Lopez; my road team, Gary Monroe, Lew Oliver, and Derek Robles! Thanks also to my managers Michael Rotenberg and Dave Becky, my agent Nick Nuciforo, my dude Kensation Johnson, and my right-hand Sonya Vaughn. Thank you, Molly Gendell, Anwesha Basu, and Kayleigh George. Love to my family: my children, Ryan, Kyle, and Tyler, and my wife, LaDonna Hughley.